Who You Are Being

By

Brad & Kasey Wallis

The Teachings of Julius

Who You Are Being
By Brad and Kasey Wallis

© Copyright 2019 by Brad and Kasey Wallis

All rights reserved. No part of this book may be reproduced in any manner whatsoever, nor may it be stored in a retrieval system, transmitted, or otherwise copied for public or private use, without written permission other than "fair use" as brief quotations embodied in articles and reviews.

Contents

Introduction 7

One~ The Creation Process 17

Two~ Human's Beginnings 30

Three~ Light Beings and Spirit Energy 43

Four~ The Human Experience 55

Five~ Conscious Creative Energy 66

Six~ Must We Have a Brain to Have a Thought? 77

Seven~ Thought is Thought! 88

Eight~ Inspirational Thoughts and What Inspires You 101

Nine~ Where Does the Ego Fit in All of This? 114

Ten~ How Many Experiences Do You Have in a Moment? 121

Eleven~ Through Broad Expansion the Spirit and Soul Grow 137

Twelve~ Your Relationship with Life's Experiences 150

Thirteen~ What Is Your Current State of Beingness? .. 157

Fourteen~ Do You Find Joy in Every Moment? 166

Fifteen~ The Pool of Thought 178

Sixteen~ Your Memory and The Pool of Thought 187

Seventeen~ Reflection and Possibilities 196

Eighteen~ Are You a Doer or a Don't-Er? 206

Nineteen~ Boredom and Getting Frustrated 216

Twenty~ Potential and Possibility 230

Twenty-One~ Things That Affect You Emotionally 247

Twenty-Two~ What Affects Your Experiences in Any Given Moment? 260

Twenty-Three~ Circumstantial Beings and Dimensions 280

Twenty-Four~ How Do You Master Your Teachings? .. 289

Twenty-Five~ Questions Humans Always Ask 298

Conclusion~ By Julius 310

Introduction

In the eternal moment of Now, the teachings of Julius are being given and heard in many lifetimes. With dramatic flair, Julius made their presence known in this lifetime during my near-death experience in 2008. It triggered the remembrance of the eternal bond we share and the work we do. Since then, their teachings have transformed not only me, but all of Julius' students. This book is my effort to share with you a crucial portion of all that has benefited so many so greatly.

Prior to my near-death experience, I had sustained a brain injury in an accident. I was prescribed a powerful sleeping medication due to sleep issues related to the brain injury. These sleeping pills were, of course, designed to allow me recuperative sleep that was vital for my recovery. They did far more than that on that unforgettable day in 2008, when I was catapulted into an incredible, life-changing, out-of-body experience. It set in motion a chain of events that would unleash a wave of enlightening information and guidance for ascension for all human beings who were ready and calling for it. The teachings of Julius had arrived!

At that time, Kasey was not my wife. We were,

in fact, just beginning to form a special friendship. That particular day I had had what I perceived to be a very hard day. I rang Kasey at around 4 p.m. and told her that I was going to take a sleeping pill and go to bed. Having approximately 12-14 hours of sleep at that time was normal for my recovery. I don't have a clear recollection of what happened after that till I found myself in an out-of-body experience, so I will allow Kasey to fill in at this point..........

Brad had spoken to me at 4 p.m. when I was picking up my daughter from school. Knowing that he would soon be asleep, my daughter and I ran errands, got something to eat, and had planned on staying at our condominium for the evening. At around 6 p.m., I had a strong urge to go to Brad's home, (it is approximately 30 miles from town). I felt that perhaps I needed to check on him because of some rough issues we were dealing with at the time. It was January and therefore very dark as my daughter and I arrived at Brad's property around 7 p.m.

There are two homes on Brad's property, the main house that was under reconstruction at the time, and a guest house that we usually stayed in. Brad was not in the guest house when we arrived, and the main house was dark because very few outlets were functioning. I thought Brad had fallen asleep in the main house and proceeded to make dinner for my daughter. I decided to leave Brad to his sleep.

At approximately 7:30 p.m., I again got an uncontrollable urge to check on Brad. I felt something was very wrong, there was an increasing sense of impending doom.

Suddenly, it became urgent to find Brad. My daughter and I went to the main house and found it cold and dark. Not being able to switch a light on, we crawled along the floor and reached the bedroom. Brad was not there. I told my daughter to close her eyes and listen. That was when we heard a gurgling sound coming from the direction of the bathroom. We found Brad lying unconscious between two unfinished walls. I immediately began CPR.

We made the 911 call for emergency assistance, and I continued CPR until the medical team arrived. As they transported Brad, the police officer asked about any medications Brad was on and we found the bottle of sleeping pills - empty. I knew it was a new prescription and seeing that empty bottle made us realize that he had taken several pills. Brain injury patients sometimes resort to repetitive actions without any recollection of what they have done previously.

During my application of CPR, Brad had his out-of-body experience, I will let him continue...

I became aware that I had left my body and was floating above it, watching Kasey perform CPR.

And then in a fluid transition, I became aware of the most indescribable sounds and colors. It was all in such a vast infinity of pure love. The light seemed to take on a group of forms and communicated with me through emotions. I felt a touch. And with that touch came recognition. I knew them.

I was met by Julius, a collective group of High Light Beings. I will not go into a detailed account because much of what I experienced is difficult to express within the limitations of the human language. Holding me in their embrace, they showed me flashes of my life and the past. They began to explain the goings on of the Universe and how I play into my own existence here on earth. My encounter with "My Group" continued all the while I was being transported to the hospital and beyond. During this time, I reached heights of inspiration that I truly cannot put into words. I was taken to places and shown things. I was told that this group had been with me in many lifetimes in physical and non-physical form and would always be with me. They asked me if I wanted to stay on earth and continue my human experience. I agreed but asked if they would continue their interactions with me. They assured me that someone was already in place to help me with that process. And with that reassurance, I reentered my body.

I was gone 8 hours and when I woke up in my hospital room, Kasey was there. She immediately began talking to me in a manner that resembled my recent conversation with my Group, and I knew she would be the one to help me have continue to interact with them.

The name 'Julius' was given to the Group because of a lifetime I shared with one of these beings, who was named Julius in that lifetime.

My wife, Kasey, is a channel. She allows entities or beings or spirits to use her body to communicate information. And she was now allowing her body to facilitate contact with the Group. She began to regularly allow this exchange and the conversations that came pouring out to me changed our lives.

Our books are an effort to give the teachings of Julius to the world in written form. They contain information that has been provided to us by the Group in the last eight plus years of ongoing teachings and private conversations.

The teachings of Julius hold the vast potential and energy of transformation because they once lived on this realm, experienced it to the fullest, its challenges as well as its joys, mastered it and ascended off it. Therefore, they have complete understanding of what it is to be human, our joys, our sorrows and how to provide that clarity and guidance that we so desperately seek in our times of turmoil, of helplessness and confusion. They come in answer to our call to learn how to master the human experience and know ourselves as we really are – the magnificence of Source. This book is about bringing you back to that remembrance. This ultimate truth is the foundation of your beingness.

"Who You Are Being" is a very powerful message and teaching given by these ascended masters to help you and me master our experience on this physical realm. It begins with the extremely important, foundational understanding that I began with. Many, many students have found that it was this understanding that gave their journey the impetus and depth they had long been searching for. This understanding is based on crystal clear information and truths that sweep away the mysteries and myths and help you remember who you are, how you came to be on this earthly realm and what you are doing in it.

Who you are being is the golden key to an

inspirational existence! It is about you, your essence and letting that essence make the fulfilling waves in your life. Perhaps you will start with smaller waves of meeting your immediate concerns and then move on to the higher waves of previously unimaginable heights – all of it possible and probable because of who you are being. All of it probable because who you are is Source and as Source you hold all potential to be and do anything that you desire. The information in this book will help you realize that potential, turn it into reality and demonstrate the miracles that are yours for the making.

After I started to write, I realized that this book will be expanded upon time and again over the years as my understanding and knowledge grows. I invite you to learn and grow with me, as more expanded truths become a part of me and I bring them into print.

I often sit back and ask myself if my life would have been different or how it would have turned out if I had been given this knowledge earlier in my life. I am still trying to master all the concepts I talk about in this book, though I have come a long way from the days of my brain injury when doctors told me all I would be good for is pulling weeds. Understanding the powerful concept of who I was being and consciously allowing it helped and healed me every step of the way to my recovery.

It has not been just a physical recovery. The expansion of my being continues, and the sheer exhilaration and joy of this eternal journey urges me to reach out, to share, to touch all who wish to know, for in ultimate reality, we are all One.

You as a reader need to know that my frustrations are a lot like yours because we are all sharing the physical experience. Kasey and I often get frustrated with life's little teaching moments and then we move on with a laugh. We are learning to tread lightly through the warp and the weft of this many-layered, fascinating world of illusion.

As you read, take the time to ask yourself questions. Ponder over the principles. See how they fit or can be used in the experiences of your life. Have fun with the book. If there is something you can't quite understand, lay the book down and come back to it after a few days. Read the book as many times as you feel inspired to. You will find that with each reading, your knowing and absorption of these truths will deepen and expand.

These are teachings of self-empowerment.

They inspire, expedite, expand each person's knowing of their own eternal truth on their conscious, awakened journey. It is that magic and that promise that has prompted you to pick up this book. May you be transformed, and may you inspire others through the powerful demonstration of your truth! As it will be!

To learn more about this channeled information and teachings, please visit our website www.expandwithjulius.com. Kasey and I hold regular classes every month in which Julius gives in-depth information and guidance on subjects that are highly relevant to the human race. We also offer live events so that audiences can experience in person the infinite wisdom, compassion and love that is Julius, as well as their extremely high energy frequency.

Contact us if you have further inquiries. We are always happy to hear from you and our assistants are available to help you.

Brad Wallis

One ~
The Creation Process

Do We Have the Ability to Create Again?

We want to begin these readings with the first concept of creation. In your previous teachings through religious indoctrinated teachings you were led to believe that first there was "The Word." The word of GOD as it is referred to in the Bible. But we want to tell you that the concept is an incomplete truth. We want to begin this teaching with a new concept of creation. We will tell you that in the beginning there was thought. In the beginning of all the universe and galaxy and possibility of all things, there was only SOURCE, and it thought unto itself.

This gave way to contemplative thought. Contemplating thought means giving emotion to a thought. By adding emotion to a thought, you have slowed down the thought process, for you have given it more time or more consideration.

SOURCE slowed the contemplative thought down a bit further, and it began to collect particles of light. This process took quite a while in what would be measured in linear time on this earth. Light danced upon the heavens and through space, for by just being part of a new experience, SOURCE found great joy in itself.

We will tell you that you are light. You are light beings. For when light was attached to thought, a new creative being was born. As light beings you spent such a long-time dancing and playing in space, moving, listening, making pictures with light, making sound from light, just being the light as it were.

From light, SOURCE continued to slow its energy down, and you collected positive and negative ions to create electrum. Electrum slowed down and collected matter, then form. You are the light beings that created electrum, then matter, and then form, and thus the creative process is complete.

You are the very being from SOURCE that created it all, adding details and imagination to all that exists.

We know that this concept may be difficult for

some to grasp because you have always been taught that you are separate from SOURCE, that you are here according to some great plan of SOURCE, and most of all that you must follow some rituals to return to SOURCE, but these are false teachings.

Let's go back in time a little bit. No, let's go all the way back to the beginning of all that there was. Let's imagine just what SOURCE was thinking when all things came about. Let's talk about all that there was, all that there is, and all that happened in the very beginning. We are talking about the creation. Not just manifestation, but creation itself.

What started the creation process? By understanding the creation process you can soon realize that by using the process, you yourself can create things in your own life.

SOURCE is thought! It is pure thought! By repeating this concept over a few times, you can begin to grasp how expansive it is. Thought is all possibility, it is all encompassing, it is ever expansive, and never ending. Therefore, SOURCE is thought.

Putting emotion to thought is contemplated thought or putting a thought into motion. One must contemplate something to create or attach energy to a thought. The contemplation creates momentum to a thought. So, SOURCE is thought, and SOURCE decided to turn it into movement and contemplate itself.

The written book of all books says, *"First there was word,"* however that is not quite true. You cannot have a word without a thought! Contemplation slows thought down and creates light.

Humanoids are the particles of light, or what is referred to as light beings. We are the particles of light, or particles of contemplated thought, and therefore particles of SOURCE.

Light, then, with the continuation of contemplation of the same thought, as well as more expansive thoughts, begins to slow the energy down, and light turns into electromagnetic currents, or electricity. The positive and negative ions that flow through electricity create dense matter. The dense matter then turns into form, and that is the process of creation.

All of that takes place when you hold onto contemplation of an idea! By contemplating something, you are adding an emotion to a thought.

You now have a feeling about a thought. You now have another idea about that thought. You are putting action onto a thought. SOURCE is pure thought! Light beings add the energy and the emotions that cause the creation process! So light beings are the creative process of SOURCE! Light beings are what created the universe and everything that you see! All those things are not only thoughts, but also emotions of those thoughts! That is what is the creative process, and from that point, all things begin.

Light beings attached gases to light particles to create universes and galaxies and suns. From the suns came the planets and the comets and the asteroids. Those are all light particles of the sun, and the sun is a light, and they are contemplated thought of the sun, which starts the creation process once again of everything that you see.

Earth then was created, and from form the next thing that light beings began to work on were patterns. It took eons for patterns to be developed; colorations and patterns were attached to the planets from the gases in the dense molecules on the planet. Some of the things that were created were plants and organic matter, and insects and fungi. All these things are thought with contemplation attached to it, or an emotion attached to it. Light electricity, positive and negative ions, and electro-magnetic matter form patterns.

Light beings were the last things to manifest themselves into a form because they realized that by remaining just light beings, they could not experience that which they had created on the plane of demonstration. How could one experience a three-dimensional form without being three-dimensional themselves? They had to be able to smell, touch, taste, feel, and sense. To do that, they had to take on a form that would allow themselves to do that. Otherwise, thought and light passes through the form, and it doesn't experience it. Light beings must attract matter to pure thought energy for that energy to experience anything that holds a form. That's what SOURCE is doing; It is experiencing itself as pure thought manifested and created into matter.

Through the formation of creatures and matter, the very first humanoid form that was created by light beings was neither male nor female. It had no exterior genitals; rather they were internal. Those early creatures were basically cloned. Through the cloning of each other, there were no mixed genes in the beginning. There was no reproductive process. It was only a cloning process. Because each light being was just duplicating the humanoid form, energy was merely trying to experience itself, which was the creation process.

Through the process of the formations of the light beings, higher energy beings were created. Through that process, all things exist at the same time, which is the eternal moment of now. High-energy light beings are the highest formation of their own evolutionary process. They have the appearance of coming before you, that you are part of all humanoid formation and the evolutionary process of itself.

So, we have just created the question of all things creating at the same time. What if the evolutionary process is not as we have been led to believe? What if the progression process works differently?

The first beings that came to this earthly realm were very simple, and they were highly intelligent in the remembrance of who they were. They existed for a long time because they were still so connected to the knowing of themselves as SOURCE. They did not give into the illusion of separation. They had memory of the absolute continuum of the creative process. In other words, they were connected more to the creative process than to this earthly illusionary process.

In the beginning, when man created itself, light energy beings created animals and things that lived on this plane before humanoid forms took place here. Light beings formed themselves last because they realized that they had to take a form to experience all that they had created. The first human forms were very rough and very simplistic; they were not very beautiful. Where the problem creeps in is when humanoids that are on this planet, or light beings that are on this planet currently have the illusion that creeps into the thought process, and because of that illusion, it creates almost a reverse thought process as to the creation.

This worldly experience and everything that goes on is a reversal process instead of an ongoing cyclical pattern, which science and the experts have no answer for.

Humanoids lived for such a long time. They only had the appearance of dying when another animal killed them. When other humanoids started witnessing this, they began to believe that they could die. Fear and instinct to survive came next, and as they fell into the illusion of fear, they slowed their vibration down and the aging process started. The body began to decompose and break down. Fear brought disease and emotional distress, and the body gave into the illusion that it would die some day. That belief, after long periods of time, became part of the souls' knowing, and so that experience was born.

When light beings created all things, they would infuse their spirit into the very thing they spread their energy onto and into it.

Spirit holds the soul. The energy of spirit that is the energy of SOURCE is what holds form together had created, to help to give it life. They. That is the spirit of all things.

Not all creations have a soul because not all creations are able to attach emotion to their thoughts. Only beings that can attach emotion to thought and are able to turn thought into contemplation have souls. It is the emotion that attaches itself to the soul; these feed SOURCE its information about its expanded self.

The spirit of all things is the energy that holds form together, or the energy together, so everything that has a form has a spirit or energy that holds it together. However, a soul and spirit are not the same. That's the reason that all creative matter has a spirit to it, because when light beings were created, they infused their spirit with it to bring it to life or into the presence. It is that spirit that helped the very thing that had been created to reproduce itself and continue the evolutionary process for the very thing that had been created to work in synchronicity with its atmospheric conditions.

The light beings continued to house their spirits and move on to the next thing they were creating and infused their spirit with that soul.

All spirits are connected, and all souls are connected to SOURCE, but your soul is the collective experience that feeds SOURCE its expanding possibilities.

Does an ant have a soul? It has the ability to contemplate thought. It can process thought in any reflective manner. So yes, an ant has a soul. They can contemplate either by behavior or by instinct, and it will turn thought into a movement, which gets recorded on the soul of that being. This flows back to the original energy thought, or as we have referred to before, the river of thought, which is SOURCE, and it expands SOURCE.

So, does a rock have a soul? The rock does not have a soul because it doesn't have the ability to attach contemplated thought or emotion to a thought. The rock reacts to the atmospheric conditions, even though it has the spirit, which is the energy of SOURCE that holds it together.

That process has brought you to today where you experience things in the three-dimensional plane. From here you are now able, because all things have been created at this point, to interchange and continually experience your spirit or your energy formation in anything. You can choose all things, and since all things were created at the same time, beings of light particles or beings of light were created at the same time. In other words, all souls were created at the same time. There are no new souls being created. The souls just reform themselves into new manifested versions of thought. You are a light particle of the first created version of SOURCE contemplating itself. You are thought.

The light beings are the ones that created the universe. SOURCE thought of it, but light energy beings contemplated that thought. Light beings put things into motion. As a light being, you are the creators of everything!

This process continues, and it expands SOURCE, but SOURCE does not have an opinion of itself. Contemplation comes from light beings. Pure thought has no opinion, but contemplation of the thought has opinions or emotions. Therefore, SOURCE doesn't have an opinion about itself. It just is. Light beings have the opinions.

What are you doing in your life or in your experience here on this plane? The answer is experiencing everything here that you have created.

Recognizing that everything that you do, if you have contemplated thought attached to it, affects your being; it is the contemplation that is the effective process. A lot of people do without thinking. Your beingness is your contemplation of yourself!

Who are you in every moment of every action of your experience? What is your awareness? What is your contemplated thought? Has reaction taken over and are you just acting? Have you left the creative process behind you?

Wake yourself up and realize the powerful being that you are! Awaken to your being!

Two ~
Human's Beginnings

Do We Remember How It All Began?

When humans and light beings came to this plane, they could remember who they were. They stayed on this plane for a long period of time. Their lifespans were long. References that are made in biblical text refer to beings that lived for hundreds of years in age; they only left this plane when they got killed. They didn't die from a disease because they were so connected. There was nothing that manifested itself in the body into disease, illness, or even an aging process because aging is a discrepancy of the body based on the lack of knowing that you are eternal.

So, when the body was killed, light beings would return to the plane of bliss and refocus themselves, remembering once again how fun it was to play on this plane of demonstration. This plane was referred to at that time as the plane of demonstration because in the three-dimensional realm, it demonstrates the creative possibilities to the light beings. The light beings created everything that was here. They understood that this was a demonstration of their creativity, and they created magnificent things. Big structures were created. It was a way for light beings to have fun on this plane and see who could out-create the other.

Light beings enjoyed experiencing themselves as SOURCE, and they would once again descend upon this plane to experience themselves and all that they had created. They continued to have very, very long lifespans because they were still connected to their own life beingness. However, the more that they came to play on this realm, the lower their frequency became.

The more clustered that humans got in civilizations and societies, the lower their frequencies got, and they started giving way to fear of survival because they could see that others could be harmed. So, they felt afraid—afraid of their own lives—and they started to forget their own immortality. They started to give way to the illusion that death could occur, that they could starve, and thus disease started. Diseases and illness are part of the illusion of disconnection and fear based upon the not remembering of the totality of your true-life-beingness and knowing that you are eternal.

When those humans died and forgot who they were, they didn't go to the plane of bliss, instead they went to a void. They didn't know what to think. They didn't know what to choose and they forgot about the plane of bliss. They very quickly reincarnated themselves to come back to this plane to experience again and decided that once they came back to the plane, maybe, just maybe, they would remember who they were. But the more they came back, the more they forgot and believed the illusion. The more that they separated from themselves, the more their lifespans became shorter and shorter because the fear kept creeping in.

Humans began to believe themselves as very limited beings, and the density of the illusion consumed them. They lost their true identity within the illusion, and thus the reincarnation cycle kept continuing. The cycle was not designed to be a prison for humans, but humans tend to hold themselves in a prison by not connecting to the knowingness of who they are.

Your soul houses all your beliefs, your knowing, and all your perceptions that turn into your experience. The more you doubt that you are SOURCE and do not recognize your true being as SOURCE, then from lifetime to lifetime to lifetime, this information continues to be recorded onto your soul. You carry that after this life, and it influences what you will experience after you die. You determine whether you will be reconnected to SOURCE in the light of yourself or go to a lower plane and reincarnate yourself quickly to try to give yourself the opportunity to remember who you are until you finally remember. For some it can take 20, 30, 40,000 lifetimes, and for others it only takes two because they remember very quickly.

What records onto your soul are the emotions connected to an experience. Belief turns into your knowing, and that turns into the recordings onto your soul.

You will experience that which you know when you leave this plane. Either you know that you are connected and that you are SOURCE, or you truly do not recall that connection. There is no hell or damnation; you'll just cycle yourself again. All the while you are expanding SOURCE by experiencing more and more, so SOURCE doesn't mind all of this going on—it simply accepts the is-ness of it and finds bliss in the beingness of itself.

If you begin to believe you can come back, maybe you'll figure out that this is how the expansion works. That is how religion started, people realized if they could falsify and manipulate tragedy, they could control people with fear. If you did not follow what religion suggested, it would cast spells and bad luck upon you, unless you followed the rules set out for you.

Wizardry was part of the beginning of religion. Magic and wizardry were the very beginning stages of religion. Humans were sinking deeper and deeper into the illusion. They were so fear-based that they became paranoid, they became judgmental, and these demonstrations and false teachings grabbed them. It intrigued them because they had forgotten their own beingness. They latched on to somebody else's explanation of things, and the religions became so deep-seated in their belief system, that this belief furthered the separation process. This was carried with you when you passed on, and because you believed in that, you were in what was considered a void. You would reincarnate yourself again to try it again. Can you see the cycle that is being developed here?

It is possible for human beings to live for more than 100 years in this lifetime. There is a possibility you can live for more than 200 years! You can halt any disease and cellular disintegration in your life by not giving into the aging process and by not believing that you are limited in all that you do. It is well documented in the human scheme of things that there are human beings that have healed themselves from illnesses and life-threatening diseases, and science has no answer for that. So why would it not be possible for you to change cellular disintegration in your life's existence? You can begin what is referred to as a regeneration process. If your knowing is true enough, and you are a light creative being, can you not regenerate yourself? Surely if you can create a flower, you can regenerate your own self. The problem comes with living in the illusion.

Governments, communities, societies, and religions teach death. They teach aging, they teach disease, and you are bombarded with those messages every day. You are bombarded with false teachings every day of your life, and you record it, because you think about it, and you add emotion to it.

You think about your limitations, you think about what's to come, and that's how the illusion keeps going and going. If you work on knowing yourself to be SOURCE, at some point, even if you still get into the illusion enough that you end this cycle at the 100-year mark, you can take that knowing with you. It goes much deeper than when people talk about positive thinking. Positive thinking means that you have a way of knowing yourself and that you are SOURCE.

You are the light created being that created all that there is. There is nothing that separates you from SOURCE. There is only the journey that you choose to take. There are not dogmatic rules, or rituals, or meditations, or fasting that you must do to get you there; you only need to get to the knowing.

Humans have fallen so deeply into the illusion, that they have also created other realms that are similar to this that you have gone to, to try to remember, and remind yourself of who you are, but you continually fall into the same pattern. You have fallen so deeply into the illusion that you have forgotten that you are the ones that created it! And those realms have the same type of experience. Sometimes you go to those realms, and even though it is the same result, it is very similar, until it is not!

Every soul makes it back to remembering. Every soul makes it back. Every soul does. So that is the good news; you don't need to worry that you won't make it back. You can actively participate in your journey once the knowing has been brought back to you, and once you have healed yourself.

What would you do the next time around with all the knowing of the onset? Or what if you had the choosing of the ultimate experience? Can you imagine what you would do with the knowing? Honestly, what could you imagine?

The soul can never be harmed—aside from physical harm that can kill you—you can live forever, your knowing comes from SOURCE, all your actions come from that place of knowing, and all your perceptions come from that place of knowing.

It is a never-ending expanding experience from that knowing in a continual state of bliss. We can guarantee that holding bliss in a continual state is the rejuvenating process molecularly. You would then be in a continual rejuvenation process. Bliss stagnates the aging process because of its high frequency regenerative powers. Fear degenerates, and most humans sit in fear significantly more than they sit in bliss because they live in the separation of the illusion.

It is fear that degenerates the body; stress is

the body eating itself. So, joy and bliss would be the body rejuvenating itself. The problem is humans take four steps forward and one step back, and in the end, you give way to fear. But the happier you are, the longer you live! That is a truth. If it is true bliss coming from your core beingness, and the knowing that you are SOURCE, it adds years to your life.

Some human beings ask the question, *"Why would you want to live forever?"* Humans that make that comment must not be very happy with the experience they are experiencing! They are missing what this experience is all about! Why would you not want to be in a continual state of joy? Do you believe that the reconnection back to SOURCE is a more joyful experience? If you know you are SOURCE, what does the climate matter? You should be in a continual state of joy. By being here on this plane you get to experience what you have created, and how much joy is there in that? That's why SOURCE came here!

By getting to the knowing of one's self—the true knowing of one's self—and in the knowing that you can create anything that you choose, you can get better at it, and better at it! It will come faster, and faster! That is fun, and that's what makes SOURCE expand.

Just knowing that you are not a victim, just knowing that you do not have to give in to somebody else's goings-on ought to take you to a place of joy! Relief and joy! *I am joyous that I am not a victim; I have refused to give in to that illusion! I am joyous that I do not have to follow rituals, and that I do not have to follow misinterpreted teachings; I do not have to starve myself. I do not have to sit on a mountaintop in deep meditation for years for me to connect with myself! I can do it any way that I choose! That is what makes me happy.* For heaven's sake, what else could make you happier? *I could be whole, and I could be healthy. Better yet, I am healthy, I am strong, and I am SOURCE!*

Develop that knowing so that it turns to wisdom. Once it is wisdom it is fully absorbed and accepted and no longer needs to be experienced again. It is complete. So, when you choose to leave this plane, you can reconnect to the plane of bliss immediately. You can choose your next experience in just the moment that you think it.

Can you see how that process takes a long time to get a hold of you? Can you see how it binds you? It really does bind you! Until it does not! There are souls that are starting to wake up to their connected selves. More of them are choosing other experiences as they come to the knowing and the remembering of who they are; they are shedding off the layers from their soul of fear, separation, and of not knowing. That is the term 'lightening your load!' You are getting rid of the layers that are weighing you down; you are lightening your load! You are turning it into light! Can you see that?

A lot of humans want the answers as to how this all came about: *Who are we? Why are we here? How did we get here?* The oddity is when humans give into a dogmatic, fear-based teaching more readily than the empowerment of their own creative beingness that brought them here! That is how deep the illusion of disconnection has been ingrained in them through the reincarnated process which is a long process. It has been taking place since the beginning of creation!

For a brief period, you remembered that you created things, but the illusion and the plane of demonstration came into play once you walked on this plane that we created. You began the process of giving way to the illusion. The moment that fear crept in, was the moment of instinctual behavior, and that was when humans lost themselves!

So, rejoice in the knowing! Play on this realm

and learn and grow; that is what we are here for! I am only here, and we are only here, to remind you of that!

44

Three ~
Light Beings and Spirit Energy

What if Science Can't Measure How Old You Really Are?

Now that your attention to certain matters has been piqued, let's give you some more information that will keep your mind expanding further. Humans are more than 10 million years old. Humanoids are that old. The reason that science and archaeologists can't measure back that far is because their time measurement is based on radioactive reaction. In other words, light measures the age of something. So, they're measuring back as far as they can to where the sun touched something and gave it an age.

Humanoids have existed on this plane when water still covered most of the Earth. At that time the sun's light was so diffused that there is no way of measuring back to that time because there was no radioactivity reaction or a measurement of age available. They are only able to estimate age according to when land was dominant on this Earth, and the sun touched something directly without being diffused through water. But there were humanoids alive before that time that existed on this three-dimensional plane—or this three-dimensional Earth—by existing in the water!

There was an ongoing evolutionary process. Let's explain part of that. When this Earth plane was covered in water, there were depths that would be considered depths of land that were being created that existed under the water, and humanoids existed on that land that was under the water. There are organs today that still exist in the human body that were used in your survival that date back to when humanoids lived in water.

As light beings created everything on this plane, they infused their spirit into it, and around it, which gave it the energy to hold itself together. It also breathed life into itself; even the insignificant objects that exist on this plane have a spirit to them. That spirit is in or around them. It is not a soul, and not everything has a soul. Remember that a soul goes into any type of being that is capable of emotion. Some creatures are a very low frequency, and have a very basic experience, but it nonetheless still has a soul. For instance, we've talked about the ant and its experience. Now it is a very low experience that the ant exists in, but that experience is still sending information back to SOURCE, and all that it is experiencing because SOURCE is everything.

Instinct is a contemplated thought; remember the thought process is the dividing line between what is and what isn't soul material. There are many religions on this earthly plane that believe that and teach that teaching, but once again that religious teaching gets back to a controlling of one's life, which is fear, and the controlling of an individual is fear based.

The spirit is infused in absolutely everything, and people would say, for instance, that a lawn tractor doesn't have any spirit to it! We would say it has spirit energy to it. It has all the materials that have come from the Earth, and everything that has materials to it has a form of spirit to it, but not a soul. But a spirit, now that is the difference. It is very low-energy frequency because it is very dense matter. It does have the spirit to it, and that energy transposes itself through time and all existence just like all energy does. That's why when humanoids have out-of-body or time traveling experiences, those experiences exist in that time. When a person has an experience of traveling back in time, and they recognize another person, and they recognize buildings that are current with that particular time period, they are transported back to that time due to the residue or residual energy spirit that has been left for time and all eternity of that existence! You can see it, and you can experience it to some degree because of the energy content of it. This is theoretically what an apparition is: there is a residual spirit energy that exists where they once were (ghosts and spirits are of the same philosophy and theory).

Spirit energy has a different density to it than gravity or atmosphere or oxygen or hydrogen. They not only have a different molecular structure to them, but they also have a different energy frequency and density to them. They all work in conjunction with each other. They are all different, and it is the spirit energy that holds all matter and energy together. It has been infused with life to continually progress and change itself, especially organic matter that exists here on this plane, because it works perfectly with the atmospheric conditions that exist here.

The synchronicity that was developed by the

light beings is incredible. Light beings designed it so that it would progress in a perfect marriage with all the other energy that progresses here. In its evolutionary process, its alignment coincides with the solar system. The alignment of the planets goes into that, the stars go into that, the energy vortexes go to all of that that exist. Everything that keeps it rejuvenated and restructured!

It all progresses according to the atmospheric conditions of the galaxies in the universe because everything changes, but they all work beautifully together until man alters it artificially! Then it must fight to get back into the balance or the rhythm of its original creative process! All energy requests that to take place, and that's where the conflict comes into play with the humanoids destroying their own environment, which is the struggle.

Even though humanoids are destroying their environment artificially at an enormous rate, there are more requests out in the universe that balance out the problems the humanoids create. Since all the other beings that live within this dimension need this dimension to live in, their requests are as powerful as the humanoids requests, so they balance out the universe. Everything relies upon the balance of each other to exist within this universe, and isn't that amazing? Amazing in the fact not only because of the simplicity of all of it, but the fact that humanoids are so good at screwing everything up because of the illusion! The illusion creates the fear, and thus the conflict that exists, and that is why religions don't work; humanoids are having inner emotional conflict within themselves because at the core of their soul, their soul remembers who they are, and that they are SOURCE.

Humanoids have amassed artificial information about their separateness. It is like a crustacean that has crusted over the knowing, layer after layer after layer, because after each lifetime, humanoids have given in to religious teachings, governmental teachings, society and community teachings, that tell you that you are a wretched creature, you are a sinner, you are separate from God, you are less than God, and you have to work your way back or you will be punished. Humans have believed this fear-based illusion for so long! It has continued for so long that it becomes part of your knowing, so humans continually have that same experience from lifetime to lifetime.

At the very core of your being there is the knowing of the "I Am" statement! The I am statement allows you to say to yourself that what you have been taught is wrong, and that you should not be giving into the illusion, and eventually it will surface itself. For instance: *I am an empowering, inspiring, accepting woman of light.*

It all starts with inner conflict, and the conflict is what the people recognize, so the people, or the humans, who give in to the exterior knowing, not their inner core knowing, will continually accumulate that crust. When they have a lifetime's existence, and the light starts to break through, the conflict will start in their lives, and that's when you are on the way to the knowing of your inner core. You may not get it in one lifetime; it may take several lifetimes of conflict for you to get it, and you will continually try everything that is out there looking for it. That's why so many people get buried in religions and beliefs. They are merely trying to find their inner knowing! They are trying to get back to being finally ready to give way to all the other beliefs that are out there. They are ready to go to their own knowing. Your knowing will tell you what is true for you according to your level of understanding.

Originally light beings educated you that you were SOURCE! According to the Bible, Jesus taught *I am your brother, not your Savior! I am demonstrating to you that I am SOURCE, and that you are SOURCE!* All Jesus did was love. At a time when men hated each other, and they were deep seeded in fear, there was only a survival instinct that was going on. There was a barbaric instinct happening, and the conflict was so deep that Jesus shone like a light in that time period, because everyone else was so violent. All Jesus said was, "*I am demonstrating the truth to you of your beingness.*" Men distorted and tweaked the truth and what he was saying a bit, so that they could gain control over the people, and it progressed from there. That is what religions have done today to gain control over people, and that is that crustacean process that continues in each generation.

It becomes part of your knowing when these fear-based emotions start to creep in. You start to think that life is so limited that you need so many things, and somebody might take them from you. Competition creeps in, and the profusion of misinformed beliefs that humanoids have held onto for so long become part of their knowing!

At the dawn of your light you know who you are, you know that you are SOURCE, and you cannot deny in the totality of all things that constitute your beingness. When you are in the illusionary plane of demonstration, you forget all the knowing of who you are. Even when you leave this plane and hold onto the knowing and beliefs of another religious teaching, you end up going to a plane that matches your energy frequency or your beliefs. There is still something in you that pulls you back and tells you that you are missing something in your knowingness, and it brings you back. It always brings you back. Those teachings pretty much explain everything don't they? They don't lay blame, they don't lay judgment, there is no one being superior over another, there is a lot of things that are simplified, and for those who are coming to the breaking through point, they will say those teachings are absolutely right because it began with them when the conflict started! They couldn't force themselves into the believing anymore; just by knowing that you were having to force yourself to do something, that is a resistance that is a conflict, so imagine when you are getting to the point that you realize that you are finally free!

You won't be punished. There is no hell or damnation. There is nothing that you have to live up to. Once that frees you don't you just want to fly? Sure, you are going to have speed bumps along the way, but just by holding onto that knowing you will get a little bit better each time.

The progression process is the breakthrough point, and sometimes it happens in one lifetime, and sometimes it takes more than one lifetime, but it is the breakthrough. It is the going from one extreme to the other, and that is what happens when someone tries to control you. It is when you have a breakthrough that you have a reaction to this experience, and you begin to know yourself! Through conflict one will turn to his or her own knowing. There will always be those who are still in the feeling of resistance to another's belief system. That is where conflict is born. They are still trying to bring you back to where they are! Religious teachers guilt you into feeling that where you're at is not correct, and all it really is doing is scaring the hell out of them! So, do you know what? Let's just do that. Let's literally scare the hell out of you because once the hell is gone you can expand yourself, and it scares religious teachers because there might be something going on that they're not doing right and that you are.

That is all part of the awakening process. It is the healing, if you will, of your soul's experience to the knowing of who you are and your connection to SOURCE. Once you know you can't be stopped unless you allow someone else to do that to you. Your spirit rejoices in the knowing, and all the new experiences you will begin having in your lifetime.

WELCOME! Begin rejoicing in yourself. You

are a light being! WELCOME and begin the journey.

Four ~
The Human Experience

What if the Human Experience is the Best of All of Them?

What if this human experience is the most complete out of all the experiences? What if this experience gets you as close to the possibility of source than any of the others because in this realm you get to experience everything you have created? Without a three-dimensional tangible body, you can't experience the things that you create. Have you ever thought of that?

We have spoken in the past that in other realms you move at the speed of light, and if you understand that concept, you would grasp that light moves through matter. There is nothing to stop it; therefore, there is no slowing down as there is on this realm. It's almost as if you're in a dream state. Dreaming it and experiencing it are completely different.

Humans sometimes believe that this realm is the lower of all experiences. This realm is not a lower experience; it is a slower experience. Because of the three-dimensional factor you merely get back to experience something. We have talked in the past of this realm being a slowed down experience, and that is so matter can collect, and objects can become three-dimensional. This is not the case in other frequencies that move quickly. This dimension and experience is slower because it collects matter. That's why things *matter* to you in this life.

Humans are led to believe that slow is worse than fast, but it's not. Therefore, slowing your life down and getting yourself out of the chaos of life, which is a fast-paced experience, allows you to concentrate and focus your energy and recognize experiences.

What if angels can't wait to be human? Do angels have feelings like humans do? Is that why they are always popping in and out and briefly showing themselves to you? They can't wait for this experience?

Humans have feelings based on tangible experience. Angels aren't three-dimensional, so they can't experience what we experience as humans.

Hollywood, in many of its movies and in its forms of entertainment, partially grasps this theory. Don't you think that is amazing? Or is it just mere coincidence (remembering there are no coincidences in this lifetime)? They have perceived a small glimpse of the truth, and they put it on a big screen and show it to all.

The key in the human experience is realizing what a creator you are. Humans forget this because they forgot that everything seems to be out of order. The experience becomes frustrating, sad, and out of control because of the dis-remembering. But if you understood that you created all of this, and you are experiencing, and get to experience, all of this, isn't that SOURCE in full potential?

If SOURCE is thought, is it more fun to come up with an idea, or an experience, or the reality of the events unfolding? Humans are here on this plane to conjure something up, create it, and then experience it.

Humans think that this is not the ultimate experience. Humans are always reaching for some form of a heaven or ethereal existence, and once again that is the illusion, or thought, that religion has placed in humans. You are taught that you are a wretched creature, you are born into sin, you are disconnected, you're tempted, and sin is related to being a human being. If you had been taught that you are the God of gods, what control could somebody have over you? Could you imagine the expandable potential that you would have in your life if you were taught that? Could you imagine the difference the human race would have if they got that? How would your experience change? Your perspective would drastically change. You would honor each other and respect each other because you are just as much a created being as the other being is.

When the teachers and the masters that are teaching on this plane understand each human being is at a different level in their human experience, what changes would they make in the teaching process? Could you imagine how different just the teaching process would be? Fear would drop away, and with no fear there's no end to potential, which is SOURCE!

Grasping the concept that light beings are SOURCE in action, where SOURCE is pure thought, SOURCE is experiencing itself, through us as human beings. Which is the greater sum? Or is there a greater sum? It is equal! Humans are just the manifestation of the idea; we are the product. So, which is the greater experience? Sitting around and thinking of something, or you now get to go and play with what you thought of!

What a tragedy it is for humans to be degraded to the point of not believing that you are valuable! Can you imagine SOURCE never having an experience or thought of itself? What if SOURCE never thought of itself and its potential or of its beingness? How sad it is for the human beings that don't see themselves that way. Most human beings are like this, actually!

Most human beings don't see themselves that way because they have been taught that they are separated. You have been taught that you are less than! You have been taught that you are less than even the higher beings like arch Angels. They don't get to experience thought; they are thinking that as soon as I get this experience right here, I get to ascend myself into a better experience. Wouldn't the better experience be having the knowing and coming back to experiencing it? And that is part of the doings of some of the human experiences. You continually get yourself back to that point of remembering. You do it thousands of times until you connect. Then you say to yourself, *"What in the world was I doing? How did I forget this?"*

Some humans get so frustrated; they just get fed up and leave! Many humans get frustrated and tired of this experience, and it is only because they have forgotten how to live in this experience and how to appreciate all that they have created! You now get to play in it!

Light beings, before they created the human body that allowed themselves to experience this experience, manifested themselves into everything else that they had created. They breathed life into it by adding their essence to it. They thought of the flower, they created the flower, they became the flower, but they could not experience the flower if they were not another form of matter. They could touch it and smell it and see it.

So, humans were one of the last manifested beings. They are simply a being that could experience everything the light beings had created before it. And how long did that take? It is an unmeasurable amount of time. If you think about conceptualizing let's say an automobile, and how far we have come, how long did it take to make a flower? How about the concept of the tree (the root system, the leaves, the colors, the shapes, sizes, and all the inorganic materials)? Then someone comes up with a prettier flower, and you say to yourself, *"Man, I'm going to do this again because I am going to make a prettier flower than they just made, and I'm going to make it a different color."* Then you fused energy into it.

When we refer to the fact that the light beings created everything, do you understand what we are saying? Do you honestly know what that means? Do you understand that light beings fused their energy into things? They held it enough, and slowed it down enough, to where it would hold its form. Then they would leave it, and the spirit of what was created becomes it. It's almost like fairy dust being sprinkled by Tinker Bell. Whenever Tinker Bell sprinkled fairy dust on something in a Disney program, it came to life. Where do you think the concept came from?

Imagine trying to create something that would continually reproduce itself, and each time it reproduces itself it gets better, it gets smarter, and it gets prettier. Envision the first flower, and then envision the first field of flowers, and then the next season after that, and next season after that, and those flowers fuse, and get bigger, and they create other flowers. Human beings are the same way. That is the process that human beings also went through.

The Neanderthals didn't move very fast, they

were eaten by lions, and as a result, another version was created. The blending process came into play; we became bigger, faster, more able to adapt, and we improved just like the plants did.

What if you are just coming to the realization of your powerful beingness, and now—like a person who is been in a coma for 20 years—you have a knowing of who you are, but now you must learn everything all over again? This time you're going to learn it from the point of view of the knowingness of how creative and powerful you are. Would it change your experience now that you're out of your coma? Would you have lessened out of yourself? Would you have less fear? Certainly, you have more appreciation for the other light beings that walk around you. And every single light being that is on this plane has contributed to all the construction that is here. You created something before you came here. What is it that you created? The flowers, grass, the trees, the mountains, oceans, the stars? What was your group in charge of creating? Without every single light being we wouldn't be here. Does that change your perspective a little bit?

Does that awaken you just a little bit? Do you remember? What is your favorite thing? Maybe it's the thing you created. Animals, plants, insects, mammals, fish; maybe that's why they are your favorite things. How about chocolate? Maybe that's why a scientist studies a certain area his whole life, because he was part of the creation process. Human beings are drawn to the very species that they created, and science is trying to remember how they did it! They don't get the connection to it. Do you? Science is learning how to clone things, they are going back to the cloning process, and why do you think that is? Because originally nothing reproduced; nothing had reproductive prospects. Everything was cloned. The problem is cloning does not expand, cloning is a repeat, and human beings are SOURCE, in a never-ending expanding process. So, things that were created were created to continually expand themselves. Cloning is duplication; it is not expansion. It's okay I guess if you're just wanting to come up with sheer numbers. They won't be able to reproduce, so once again you are back in the reproduction process.

Could this possibly be a repeating process because of the eternal moment of now? Are you merely trying to experience everything over again? SOURCE doesn't care. SOURCE says go ahead; you are expanding me! How much deeper in this illusion can you set yourself up for?

Getting back to the original teachings, you are

all that is, not just on this plane, but all there is. Anything that holds any form or shape came from light. Humans are the light beings; humans are the creators of all that there is. That is SOURCE experiencing itself!

SOURCE is on a never-ending, always expanding journey to everywhere! Have fun with everything you have created! Don't ever forget that other light beings and other human beings create as well. They are equal to you. Treat them as such. Now go find somebody and create something!

Five ~
Conscious Creative Energy

What do you think about the phrase "*conscious creative energy?*" It is the difference between unconscious thought verses conscious thought. It means once a thought is formed it turns into energy. It is a process of creating energy. Do you see that?

Even a thought creates an action, and every action has energy to it. Everything has energy to it. So once a thought is born and the energy is attached to it, it has the potential for manifestation depending upon the energy you attach to the thought.

In the manifestation process you first begin with thinking about something and then putting more energy to the thought. Focusing more and more energy to an idea helps create or manifest it into being. But what if the manifested thing needs continued creative energy to keep it manifested and in the illusion.

Once something is created, let's say a chair, and placed into a room, all the other energy in the room recognizes and accepts that there is a chair sitting in the room. Even energy that you're not aware of. There are beings in other dimensions around us all the time that contribute to the *conscious creative energy* that is going on, on this plane. Without you even realizing it there is energy being emitted from all the other objects in the room that contribute to the expansion of the created object. Therefore, the other objects continually contribute to the creative thought process that holds the item together and the energy of it together. If all the energy in the room acknowledges that there is a chair in the room, then that energy is constantly reinforcing its existence.

Just a thought that your ceiling is brown contributes to the ongoing energy that keeps it looking brown until all energy agrees that the color is changed, then it contributes to the knowing of the new color. Now that you know that the ceiling is brown, you always know it is brown. So, every time you look at it, it is brown. You recreate it every time you have a thought about your ceiling.

That practice is a low-energy process, because even though it took high concentrated energy to manifest the item or idea, it then holds a low frequency in order to hold matter. Remember that in the creative process first there is thought (high energy frequency), then there is contemplative thought (slowed down version of thought), then there is light (slowed down version of contemplation), then electrum (continue the slowing process), then matter and so on. You can see that all things that hold a density of matter hold a low vibration. For example, when somebody else thought about creating a piece of wood, and somebody else thought about adding a color to it, every time another person looks at it and acknowledges that it is a honey brown color, it keeps itself manifested as that. That is a high collective creative energy process.

At the same time the very item or issue or experience that holds any density of matter also emits that low frequency to keep its form.

As you look around the room and acknowledge the items in it you are adding to its vibrational existence by joining the *collective creative energy process* that is continually going on to create this illusion. Each time you recognize the illusion you reattach energy to it, you hold the illusion, and you hold the manifestation of it. That thought that you put into recognizing the 'isness' of anything that is in the illusion doesn't seem like difficult creative energy to contribute. You seem to do it so unconsciously, and yet look how powerful the *collective thought energy* is.

In the process of the thought being created, whatever really is going to be is a verb because it is in the action of taking place. Once it is manifested it becomes that thing. It is a noun. So, the process of conscious creative thought and energy is not only an action, but also a noun because it is a process of manifestation.

The act of teaching how to create through thought is difficult because of the limitations of the human language. You can't come up with enough verbiage to explain an emotion or a sense or a process because everybody is different. If I say to you, *you have exuberant energy*, what kind of energy do I have? If I say *you need to attach exuberant energy to your thought*, what does that mean? What I'm telling you is you need to get all your emotions involved, all of your positive, ecstatic, best feeling emotions behind a thought and throw them out into the universe. Put it in the universe and say *it is! It is this way that I am living the experience of this process. Thank you for bringing it to me. It is here, it is now, and it is. What does it feel like? I have achieved abundant success.*

So, what does it feel like? Stir that energy up as you are attaching it to the thought. Does that make sense? It is! It is now. It is in the moment of now; I am living the experience, I am living the feelings of knowing that the money has come, I am living in abundance, I am expanding, and it feels good. Thank you, universe, for sending this experience to me; thank you for sending this reality to me. I manifest this as my reality and experience. You are in action, and so it is.

By being conscious of your thoughts you are able to manifest the very things you put out to the universe to provide. You are doing this very thing all the time even when your unconscious thoughts are involved. That is why things don't seem to have order, or you feel like you don't have control over the illusion. If your unconscious thoughts are powerful enough to keep you in the ongoingness of the illusion unfolding around you, just imagine how powerful you would be if you turned each thought into a conscious one.

Teaching the *conscious creative energy process* to others can be a real problem since the words and the feelings of others are different from your own. When you are told to add intense emotional energy to a thought in order to speed up the manifestation process, you are victim to the interpretation of the words "intense energy." That can mean different things to different people. What you feel is one way and isn't the same feeling for another. A master teacher recognizes that and tries to get all to feel something, and then they can use the words to expand for themselves. Remember you can only ignite the truth within; it is up to the individual to progress from where they are and move on to the next experience. The human language isolates humans in their understanding and in their comprehension. Words are so limited in the human language. You go with what you have and hope that people will understand. At some point there will be advancement as to not needing words, where you will be able to express through thought alone, and you get your intention. There are few on this plane that practice that concept, and for most it is not common.

The language is difficult. It is very limiting; it is the causation of so many things that are wrong here because of misinterpretation. If you think about it, just in the writing process in putting pen to paper, for some people expression comes very well that way and it can be a better form of language. Some people have a better talent of putting their emotions to paper, but the average person loses fluctuation and emphasis on a statement, and any given statement can be taken for misinterpretation. So, interpretation is huge just through the fluctuation of expression on that statement.

Anything can come across as a compassionate statement or a threatening statement. Other beings that exist on other dimensions or realms don't communicate through talking or through a limited language. They communicate through pure thought energy and simplify the process. They have a *conscious energy output* that contributes to the expansion of all items on this plane, and so do the other items that have been created because they have a spirit or energy infused into them that contribute to the acknowledgment of the other items that matter here.

The transcending of energy is a natural process for the earth and all that grows and lives here. It is just a question of whether it is a conscious act or an unconscious act. With the energy exchange that occurs naturally in nature, and with the pushing and the pulling of energy frequency, you have growth and expansion and the holding of the illusion going on all around you. Can you imagine if all humans became consciously aware of their creative energy?

It is the same principle as collective prayer. Collective conscious energy: listen to that statement and how profound, and mostly how powerful, it is. The power of collective energy can move mountains. It moved your pyramids, or at least the stones they are made of. Collective energy can heal everything your human body and the earth needs. Crystals collect and harness these types of energies as well as rocks and sand and water. Magnets are a powerful example of the push and pull energies. They create their own energy in their magnetic pull and push. You can almost see the energy that is created that sits between the magnets; it is so thick and strong, and it almost manifests itself into matter. A trained eye can see this energy. Close your eyes and you certainly can feel this energy. Imagine what it would look like. It would feel heavy; that pull is such a heavy energy that you can almost scoop it up in your hands and wash yourself with it.

That's what they do, you know. The higher light beings wash themselves with energy. They dip their hands in it. They spread it like butter around. They drink it in. They feed themselves with it. They share it with you. If you ask, they will pour it on you;

just ask. You can share your energy with another and transfer that energy to another who is weak or in despair. You can become consciously aware of your own energy output and condense it into a beam of light and send it into another. Or you can emit it through your hands and wash over another with it. You just need focus and belief. The knowing that it is there brings it about. Just as the knowing of anything brings that thing into being. That's how you got here. The healers know all of this; the only difference is in the practice and the knowing. They have shed their fear of the process and embraced the magical forces it seems to bring. Try it! Heal yourself! We challenge you to do so. You will find it is a rather simple game. You only need to get out of fear and totally create your experience. Use your *conscious creative energy* output.

With the bringing of information comes the remembering. With the hearing and receiving of information comes knowing. All things lead to home. Imagine there is no end to the knowing and the getting familiar with yourself; to re-member yourselves, to come back to SOURCE, and then do it again because you cannot know enough of yourselves. It would be an endless, stimulating experience. Can you imagine? Well you have; that's what you are doing.

So, put your energy into intention. Put all thought into a conscious action, and you will see miracles occur. You are the most powerful beings because you are SOURCE. You can create anything you choose; just learn to be conscious of it, and it will change what matters to you.

When you think about it, no matter how much you understand or don't understand, *conscious collective energy* is used in more things than you are aware of and can be the basis for everything there is on this plane. When we begin to understand that truth and exactly what it means, then we can move on to the next lesson that we need to learn in this life.

Six ~
Must We Have a Brain to Have a Thought?

The Brain Does Not Create Thoughts!

The brain collects all the data that is being thrown around you and processes it. Your own energy source is continually putting out energy and thoughts, so you literally do not need a brain to have a thought!

Someone else's brain will eventually collect your thought and process it accordingly and then come up with an opinion of it. That's why you ultimately have the ability to tap into all the knowledge that is out there.

Have you ever wondered why certain people, let's call them high-energy beings, always want to be left alone? Why are they always out in the elements by themselves? Or why they surround themselves with individuals that have the same thought processes they do? They don't want to get caught up in all the confusion that is going on around them in society. They understand that they are able to receive more information in the quiet of the world or by even sitting in some form of element that is here on this earthly plane. They understand that the pool of thought is constantly changing, and as the pool expands, SOURCE expands, and then you expand. So why clutter up your thoughts with something that is of no value?

Remember, it is all energy created by all, and it is opinion and perception. Can you begin to see how large the creative process really is? This is an old and new idea. Hopefully I haven't lost you back at not having to have a brain!

When you begin to grasp any form of enlightenment, you are progressing in the process. Have you ever thought what a towel is experiencing on this plane? How about the shopping cart? Yes, it sounds trivial, but when I say all things it really means ALL things. The process can become stifling! When your thought is thrown into the river—or the pool of thought—what frequency was it thrown in at, and what will be attracted to it? ALL these factors contribute to who YOU are being because of what you are doing!

Energy frequency will attract likened energy frequency. For example, when, or if, you have ever pushed a magnet through a pile of sand, what happens? Likened energy particles are attracted to the magnet are they not? So why aren't all the particles that you are pushing through become collected? It is simply because they are not attracted. Ok, let's wet a piece of wood and run it through the same pile of sand. What happens then? Likened energy frequency particles are collected. Not all particles, though. Can you see that? Just what matters to the magnet or the wood is collected. This is just like our own thought process. When an energy frequency matches another energy frequency they collect, and yet there is still material in the sand pile (or should I say a different version of the sand). That is why so many people come up with different versions of the same theory! All are correct. They are just different versions with different energy. You are going to attract the particles that match your energy frequency. Have you ever thought of it that way? Are you the magnet? Are you the piece of wood? Are you a piece of paper? Or maybe you are the water droplet itself! ALL contribute to the pool. ALL are correct in their energy process. ALL have nothing to do with your brain. Yet ALL have something to do with your being! What are you in the grand pool of energy knowledge? What thought, idea, creation, is attracted to you and expands your mind, which, in turn, throws out new ideas of expansion for others? It is all added to the collective knowledge river, and it never ends.

This is the truth of all existence, and this is how existence works. It goes beyond any written teaching. It goes beyond anyone's single thought of a knowledge or understanding of the thought of creation. It is beyond any individual's comprehension level, of the depth of the contributing process, and of ALL energy! Only SOURCE has full comprehension, humans can only comprehend to a certain point. ALL this contributes to the ongoing beingness that you are. At every level your existence has the need to experience; no one is higher than the other. We all contribute according to what we comprehend and understand. That contributes to the ever-running river that flows back to the SOURCE of all things, which expands SOURCE and expands you. It is like the human heart; what do you think the human body is based upon? What do you think plants are based upon? Or an animal? Hence the term you are created in the image of SOURCE!

The brain then collects thoughts that are out in the energy atmosphere, the brain catches that thought and you as a human being immediately attach emotion to it. It may be such a small amount of emotion, that the thought doesn't impact you that much. Other times it impacts you so much it creates a lot of emotion. It is that emotion that gets registered on your soul. It's not the thought itself; it's the energy the thought creates through the emotion that is registered on your soul. Then when the soul is looking for the memory of something, it will search its database, so to speak, that went with that thought before, and that's how the floodgates come back from past memories. It's how you know what a flower is, for instance, because it triggered a certain emotion with you before. Even though you may have grown up not being told it was a flower, at some point you were told it was a flower. That flower then is emotionally attached to you in your remembrance. For some there is so much emotion attached to the flower that whenever they see or are given flowers, emotions arise, and they are let out of the human body. Thus, the human reaction to receiving flowers.

Humans have no comprehension as to how many degrees of emotion there are. Like so many other degrees in all existence, humans are only able to grasp their own emotions because it is something that happens to them. Emotions have so much energy and collect so much energy from the universe. The brain is the organ that processes all of it. Different emotions go to different parts of the brain, and that is why it is so different for everybody. Your brain is really just a big processing center for all the different types of thoughts that are out there. Each human's brain reacts and reflects what is only important or imperative to them.

Absolutely everything you have ever done, chosen, or experienced began with a thought as well as how you felt about that thought. Everything! How you felt about it was the driving force as to your action of whether you did anything about it or not. How strongly did you feel about it? It all started with you collecting an idea or a thought that is out in the energy force where everybody else is thinking of things. The more you think of, the more thoughts you throw out there, and others can pick up on that same thought. It is a hugely expansive phenomenon. Humans don't understand that because it isn't just human thought that is out there in the pool. It is all thought.

People ask the questions: *How do I become more aware of what is happening around me*, or *how do I become more aware of myself?* The first part is becoming aware of your emotions. Not just the logical ones, but also all the emotions. How do you process these emotions throughout your day? How do those emotions get registered with you? What, and how, do you feel about them? They all leave a form of residue on your soul. You learn how to behave by how well you can process these emotions and how they impact you in your life. Remember it isn't how well you control your emotions, but how you become aware of those emotions. Instead of just letting them run around you erratically without a second thought given to them, you control them by becoming more aware of what exactly is going on and how they affect you.

Now let's talk about the so-called wisdom factor in all of this. Many human beings are referred to in this lifetime as having so much wisdom. Wisdom is the knowledge applied, or should I say, it is what humans put into action. We as human beings are so consumed with everything else that goes on in our daily lives and activities that we don't realize that all these emotions are applied in all that we do.

Wisdom appears in our existence as a tunnel, or should we say what is referred to as a tunnel of wisdom. All the plans that you make in this life, and in between lifetimes experiences, whether it is you coming back as a human being, or even coming back and having the experience as a whole different type of being, when that decision is made, you descend yourself into what you would call a lifetime of experience. It is literally a tunnel! Whatever that experience might be.

Along with choosing the lifetime experience, you choose what form it is you are going to take, and that form changes with the experience you decide you want to have. It changes according to your experience, after experience. And wisdom appears as a tunnel.

Of course, it gets complicated when one is told that all experience occurs at the same time while you are making choices for your next experience. That is a very delicate balance between everything that is there, instead let's just refer to the next lifetime theory at this moment. Or should we say the next lifetime?

Remember that all things exist at the same time. There is the realm where you make possibilities and experiences for your next lifetime(s), and you get to experience your experience from previous experiences. All that exists in ultimate reality because ultimate reality is all possibility. A tunnel is an easy way to describe this phenomenon because wisdom appears this way.

When humans die, they refer to what is called the tunneling effect that they recall. All this time they forget that it is all part of the process of recalling their decisions they have made, and what effect those decisions have on their experiences here on this plane!

Let's now talk about your next choice. You decide to descend yourself into what is called your *next life's experience.* All of the decisions that you choose to experience and make affects the decisions and experiences you decide to have in order to experience what it is you decide to be or experience this time around. As you are descending yourself into that type of process, you are also fine tuning some of your decisions. What family do you decide to live in? What type of life you are going to have for yourself? What type of plant you are going to be? Can you see how many decisions one has to make? And amongst all those decisions you decide what type of being you decide to be. Within all of that you also decide how you are going to live—whether to live in ignorance, in knowledge, in pain, in suffering, in bliss. The list is endless. Each affects your state of being each time around.

What you choose to live is completely your decision. Humans forget that it is their own decisions that they have made, and that is what they are living and experiencing in each lifetime's experience. No one is responsible except you! You made the decision, or you wouldn't be living it!

Your brain merely collects all this, processes all this, and lets you experience all this according to what it is you have decided to experience this time around. Then it dumps it all into the river of knowledge so SOURCE, and you, can expand. What a hard concept it is for some to grasp, and if you think about it long enough, you can give yourself a massive headache. But for some it is the answer that they have been searching for.

Let's continue in this discussion on why we have certain types of thoughts, and inspirational thoughts, because the thoughts we have affect our beingness more than we can understand.

Seven ~

Thought is Thought!

Have You Ever Wondered About That?

Thought is SOURCE in its purest form. It is very difficult for human beings to understand this. If you play in the three-dimensional realm, and if you have decided to descend yourself onto this plane to play as a three-dimensional being so that you can experience all things three-dimensional, your frequency, or your vibration, is the same as other three-dimensional beings that are here on this realm. In other words, you must hold a certain vibration, so your body can keep its three-dimensional form.

Your consciousness can vibrate at a higher vibration, but your body will still vibrate at the same vibration as the three-dimensional beings and forms that are here on this earthly realm. What makes you think, or what makes you feel, that you are better than any three-dimensional thing that is in this three-dimensional world? If you are three-sided as a human being, and the tree that sits at the city park is three-sided or dimensional, or if the vehicle you drive is three-sided or dimensional, what makes you believe that you are any better than they are? You are all three-dimensional! You all have a three-dimensional form. Now the difference is this: does the tree or the vehicle that you drive think in ultimate reality? No. We are not dealing with ultimate reality!

The mere fact that they have a conscious awareness of their form or their thought would be getting too deep in our subject matter, and that is not what we are talking about. That is for another discussion at a later date.

What this shows is that you and the other three-dimensional resources or beings that have created themselves, all contribute to the energy that all things here on this earthly plane are as three-dimensional objects. Whether it is organic or inorganic, its energy contributes to the illusion and to your experience. It should command the same respect that you command from the universe for your presence and existence.

Until you get yourself into a state of

appreciation where you hold all energy in the same aspect and in the same highest state of admiration and gratitude and acknowledgment, you will not grow past playing in the three-dimensional realm, or any other lower realms. You would not be able to take yourself back to the seventh dimension in heaven and the connectivity back to SOURCE.

This is a hard truth! Your soul has set itself up in for this journey here. There is so much to be accomplished! *How can I get myself back? How can I get myself into the pure state of where SOURCE is?* The true answer is: let yourself be open to all of that that is made available to you and all of possibility! All that makes way to all of your previous assumptions, teachings, and beliefs that are nothing more than someone else's idea and illusion that sits around you. Can you do that in any moment? It's going to the place knowing; knowing that you are connected to all things no higher or lower than all things. Hold yourself in the highest state of possibility!

The human ego detaches itself from the truth because of the illusion. They detach because of the doing in their lives. They detach because they have lost who it is they are being. Are you beginning to understand this concept in your life's existence?

So, when we start talking about thought being thought, there is a difference between thought and contemplated thought.

Thought is SOURCE, and SOURCE is all thought, which is all possibilities. I know that that subject is repeated, but that is because the subject really needs to be grasped! Throughout this dialogue that will be repeated: Thought is SOURCE! It is a thrown-out possibility. Now we are not talking about an idea because an idea is the mind grabbing onto a thought and the mind contemplates it. We are talking about pure possibility and pure thought.

A thought is different than the contemplated thought, or an idea. Once you contemplate thought, then you can conjure an idea from that contemplated thought. For example, you are snow skiing on the side of a mountain, and in the process of snow skiing you realize that you could start a business that has something to do with the snow skiing industry. That idea is formed from your contemplated thought. Contemplation is putting more energy, or slowed down energy, to your thought. Thought moves at the highest rate of possibility. It is SOURCE. It is the beginning SOURCE of all things. When you contemplate thought you grab it, and you add or slow down its energy as you grab it, and you hold it, so you have slowed its energy down.

Thought always comes first. All thought is created, or was created, at the same time. This is one of those mind-bending realities that I like to occasionally toss into a discussion. Thought is SOURCE acknowledging itself and choosing to create itself in a continual existence that never ends. When a human being thinks, or they have a thought when dealing with the term "thought is thought," what do they think about? What do they contemplate? What do you focus on that is adding different forms of energy to the pool of thought?

The pool of thought gives us all possibilities because all thought exists in the pool of thought. That's why when it is said that there is nothing new that can be thought about or that can be created, we are merely saying you just haven't tapped into it yet, and it seems new to you because you have detached yourself from all previous consciousness and the knowing that you are connected to all thought at all times. There really isn't a learning process; it's a remembering process. You remembered everything the minute you thought of yourself since you are SOURCE thinking of yourself now.

Now beyond that concept, we are speaking of your conscious awareness, the goings-on, and the inner beingness of your soul. This is carried by the spirit. During your humanoid experience, what you think about and contemplate grows ideas, and then from your experience all your humanoid experiences are developed. That is your doing.

A lot of people do discover a big portion of their beingness by the things that they do; however, doing it that way is the long route. If you were connected to yourself from the very beginning, and you were connected to your beingness, your doings would never falter because they would be direct actions of your beingness instead of filtering through a whole bunch of doings going on in your life. You then would be discovering who your beingness is. There would never be anything but pure state of consciousness if your beingness awareness came first, and then your actions were an expression of your beingness.

A lot of people's doings are not expressions of their own beingness. A lot of people do for other people's intentions and ideas and beingness. They're almost like blind actions; they're not completely blind actions, but in your conscious state, if you are not aware of your beingness in all that you do, then they seem to be blind actions, and more often than not, reactions to something else. If you were creating the moment as a reflection of your beingness, then it becomes your doing. All these things go on in the human experience, and for many humans none of that even goes on since they are so lost in the illusion. As such, they walk blindly and walk so disconnected.

You see and recognize those people as well. They are very easy to spot, and they are definitely the souls who like to control others. They are dissuaded, and they are disconnected. For the human to start becoming aware they must decide that along their journey of their doingness on this plane and the artificial absorption of the illusion, somewhere in there is a higher consciousness that will bring them to a state of awareness of their beingness.

How do we go about that? There are so many levels of consciousness to be absorbed and recognized and appreciated on this worldly realm. Before you really grasp anything in your attempt to recognize your beingness, do you start by recognizing your own true beingness and never-ending possibilities of expansion? Then do you work your way into the recognition of all things around you and their contribution and energy frequency? All are a contribution to the illusion and experience of your existence. Do you realize that every form of matter has its own energy collection to it, and therefore, is on or is in a contributing state that adds to your consciousness and awareness? Do you recognize the other consciousness first before discovering all of your own inner self? One needs to understand that you have to have awareness of both! That's the question that comes first!

Do you find full conscious awareness of your own eternal being first, and then open yourself up to appreciation of all levels of beings and consciousness that exist? Do you understand that all contribute to your level of existence around you? Or is it the other way around?

Some people start to think: *"My goodness! I believe that has energy to it. How does that relate to the ongoing eternal existence of my being?"* It really doesn't matter. You cannot be one-sided. You must understand that all things do come into play. It can't only be a consciousness of self without giving awareness to all consciousness around you. Even if that means you begin to recognize inorganic matter that exists around you because the inorganic matter has energy that holds itself together as well. For example, it's not Elmer's glue that holds your television set together. There is energy or a spirit that holds that matter together. The glue can hold the form together that will create the television set, but the television's own spirit holds the matter together.

That's what science can't get. They acknowledge that there is something that holds the universe, the galaxies, the planets, the meteors, and the comets all together. There is something that is holding all the dark matter together. It is the spirit that is SOURCE that holds it all together. Science is missing that link. Science is calling the spirit dark matter, but that is incorrect. The spirit holds dark matter together, and it gives everything form. Science can even measure it; they can measure an energy that exists there, and science continues to call it dark matter, but it is not dark matter. It is spirit. Scientists cannot bring themselves into the concept that there simply is an energy that they cannot explain, that is the energy of all beingness, or thought that is SOURCE. Science recognizes a lot of it. They can continue to measure energy, they can keep measuring different forms of energy, but they won't concede the point that there is an energy of spirit that collectively holds and houses everything.

What then is the difference between the soul and the spirit? The *soul* resides deep in the human consciousness. The soul is at a superconscious level, and it is the collection of all experience. It is like the gigabytes in the computer; it is that internal sweet spot that collects all the information of not only your existence or what you would perceive to be your own personal experience or existence, but it is all information collected and sent back to SOURCE. So, it is the grand housing of experience and information and perception and all those things. *Spirit* is the energy that is SOURCE and connects all things together. It carries every form of matter and every form of contemplated thought and houses it.

Your soul resides deep inside your superconscious awareness, and it resides deep inside the human body. The spirit carries you around; some people perceive that to be what your aura appears like. They are not the same thing, but if that's where your mind goes you can remember that spirit is the aura energy that carries you around. As you ascend out of your body, your spirit leaves easily, but the soul gets pulled from the body by the spirit. It's almost like pulling a core out of an apple or pitting an olive.

There is a connection between the spirit and

the soul, and when you sleep your spirit leaves your body, but the soul remains with the three-dimensional body. Spirit can feed the soul information based upon the experience it is having because it never completely leaves the body since the spirit connects all things at all times. There is never a full disconnection. That is the difference between the soul and the spirit and how it all works together for your gaining of your experience for your level of awareness and your activity of beingness that is SOURCE.

Getting back to thought and its process in all of this, consider it to be the light fragments that is SOURCE. During the human experience it is your brain that taps into the pool of thought. The brain is the receiver that triggers all the process. The brain collects the light fragments that came from contemplated thought, and your soul is a fragment of that light. Human beings are pure light energy beings. It is the internal light that exists inside of you. That is the flame that is the light that we refer to when we say *go to your core, go to your light being,* or *go to your flame*. That is you; it is truly your existence. You carry that light through all your types of existence. You always carry that light because you are a light being. Some beings choose to be higher light beings, and some choose to be lower light beings, but all are light beings. Some stay in pure light form, and they teach. They are called pure light-energy beings. They do not hold a three-dimensional body. Others, like yourself, who choose to be three-dimensional realize that it all begins with a thought.

Most humanoids that walk on this plane do not remember their spirit and soul are SOURCE. They have been so discouraged by the controlled teachings given by those who live in a pure state of fear or disconnection that they struggle to get that the goings on here are too difficult to manage.

It can be an arduous task, we know, to breaking through these un-truths and the bonds that keep you not only in this hologram, but, even worse, keep you in your disconnection to self. By opening your soul and opening your mind's blocks against all possibility, you can begin the process for remembering.

These teachings intended to remind you. These teachings are reminders of your powerful being, that you are SOURCE, and that if you can just start to lower your walls and peek over the top to the light that is showing, you can begin to feel the joy and bliss of connection.

This process takes courage, it takes patience, and it takes a form of discipline. Each time you find yourself in fear and disconnection or not believing in yourself, you must bring yourself back. In the illusion one can get so stuck that giving into the illusion seems easier, but once you experience the joy of connection, you will remember there is more. Think about it. It is all in your thoughts.

Eight ~
Inspirational Thoughts and What Inspires You

When you have an inspirational thought, or you receive a thought that inspires you, have you ever wondered if you had sent that thought or idea to yourself? Could that thought be based upon something you should have done, but didn't do, in a previous lifetime? Are you inspired to follow that thought or try again this time around now that you are receiving that thought? This time you'd know how to do it or how to go about doing it.

Let's consider what the soul and the spirit do from lifetime to lifetime, and how it is that it is so easy to do certain things in your life without feeling that you must have any practice or schooling at it. What value would you get in this human existence if you had previous lifetimes of experience to help you?

We have already talked about how the soul collects experience, and how you are able to tap into experience if you are willing and able to do so.

Beyond that, though, what tools do you get to use from your previous experience?

We would tell you that when you do something that you have prior experience with, and somebody comes along who doesn't know how to do it, you would usually help them with what you know how to do, right? You would at least try to share some of your knowledge with them on the subject, correct?

What if you were the same soul over again that had previous life experience on a subject? You may have missed the subject in the past, but you are inspiring yourself this time around to tackle and accomplish the subject this go around. This is based upon your previous life's experience. So, what is it that inspires you then? What causes you to feel inspiration toward something?

Some people would merely say that what someone else does inspires them, or what someone does inspires them to try the same thing! It triggers something inside you, and that is where the inspiration comes from! Well let's throw this argument out there: are you sure that it is not you showing your own self that very thought? Are you sending yourself a message of the potential of what you had previously accomplished? Maybe it is that *I*

AM statement that you sent out into the universe. You wanted to accomplish that very thing but didn't, so this time around you are going to send your own self inspiration and information on how to attain it. Does that sound too far-fetched?

Inspiration comes from many, many venues. It can be a driving force for somebody, and it can be a downer for others. For those who are driven we would ask: why is it that you are so driven about a certain thing? Why are you so driven to have this career? What drives you in that direction? Some will say, *"Well it is what my father or mother did,"* or, *"It has been this way as long as I can remember in this family, so we all do it!"* Where does that drive come from? Does it come from previous life experience? Is it your own self sending you messengers—or *runners* as we refer to them?

What if, in between lifetimes, you have the ability to reinsert yourself into the lifetime of a loved one and replay a role that was valuable to you? You may experience change due to actions that were forthcoming. Let's give you an example. Your best friend passes away, and in trying to communicate with you, you as a human being sit and ponder memories of your childhood and recall a special friend or someone who inspires you. Perhaps the person who has passed reinserts his or herself as the residue of the friend of your previous memory who re-inspires you and changes your forthcoming actions. Or maybe they talk to you in a certain way. They say, *"Man, I remember a certain person when I was young, and this was the relationship we had, and isn't it funny that they remind me of this certain person who has passed?"* Suddenly there is a window created by that person that allows another way of communicating with you through previous memory by reinserting and validating themselves by a previous memory. That might sound tricky to you. It could be as simple as that recurring dream that you have.

How many ways can a soul break itself up and reinsert itself into your dreams or thoughts before you realize it is you? It may inspire you, warn you, or may even guide you. It is all forms of communication, right? The best form of communication is through the mind, emotions, memories, dreams, and foresights; those are the best methods of communication because, by inserting a dream or idea in a memory, there is no lack of communication since you have inserted the experience yourself.

For most, if not all of us, we were happy when we used to run on the beach and play. If I can implant that memory in you, into your brain, or into your superconscious mind, there is no need for the communication. I don't even have to tell you we were happy because you feel the happiness of the memory. You recall the memory and the communication and what it felt like. What we are talking about is insertion. It is a wonderful way to communicate. There are no words needed.

How do you communicate to somebody how you feel, compared to how they feel, about any one subject matter or experience? For instance, I can tell you that I love you, but what does that mean to you? It is guaranteed that the other person will not feel the same love. Do you see the same color that I do? If I can't take the color out of my eyes and put it into yours, how do you know it is the same color?

A great way that a soul communicates with you as it is passing away is by the insertion process. Sometimes that communication is merely a spark of an idea or a memory in you of an experience that you had. All he or she is doing is reinserting him or herself as that person to spark that memory. That memory is what passes on the communication with you. They are merely using all tools that are available to them. The tools that they have available to them once they have passed is what is left with you. So, what's in there?

Memories are in there, actions are in there, feelings are in there, and the best way for me to communicate with you is to get into you! How do I insert myself into your soul in order to communicate with you? Most humans wait for a three-dimensional ghost to appear and have a conversation with them. Do you honestly believe that they need that to communicate? They are now totally expanded by emotions, theories, thoughts, and creative energy. So how do you think I am going to communicate with you? Why would I go back to the square wheel when I have rocket jets to send you! That's why so many humans miss the communication. They are always stuck on the way you communicate in the three-dimensional form. That person is no longer three-dimensional! How are they going to communicate with you? It is by insertion! I am going to get into you! I certainly am going to get into your dreams because that is the easy way to do it.

Dream state is a very entry-level form of frequency of energy. It is very easy for an entity to insert themselves into your dreams because it is what is referred to as entry-level. This is because of the frequency that it emits. Do you want a heavier entry? Memory overhaul! I am going to tweak your memory by inserting myself into the action of another in your memory bank. Re-stimulate the possibility of thoughts and emotions and actions in you. It is a much better way to communicate with you. It has nothing to do with speaking through words. That's why so many people miss the communication. They don't understand where it is coming from! Unless they do. Then they won't miss it!

There are many humans who have children who have passed, and they have a much broader sense of who that soul was after it passes than when it was limited to the three-dimensional body and spoken words. Now they can feel them communicating. They get a sense or a feel for that soul because that soul can insert itself in you. It is not in an invasive way, but in a communicative, loving, and sharing way. How much communication do you miss? We can absolutely guarantee all humans miss communication! What is it you have missed? If you have received the information, have you had a conscious register as to the knowledge that you missed? Have you had inspirational thoughts? Have you had inspirational actions? Have you had an insertion of a spirit, or even SOURCE, in your life, into your memory banks, into your spirit, into your outlook, or into your perspective? Most humans can't hold onto its grasp; do try to hold onto it! It opens up a whole new form of communication to you, and it changes your beingness when you get it.

Where do your thoughts come from? Now that is a good question most humans don't ask themselves! Let's imagine for a moment you are a being that has the whole universe at your disposal. There are no boundaries or limitations. Anything you can think of you can do. What would you do? What would you do for the people that you have left behind? How would you help them? Would you stay and help, or would you just go? Does it depend upon how connected to that person you were? Or is it an answering of a calling if you will? Do those who have passed ache for communication? Or are you aching for that communication? Do they want to lose touch with you, or do you not want to lose touch with them?

Your perspective is your reality, and what is needed will be. Those who understand the process understand that it is what you are being and not what you are doing! There is an eternal concept: *It is not what you are doing, but what you are being! So, who are you being?*

It really doesn't matter what you are doing as long as you are being. What version of SOURCE are you being? Can you look back at all those times and remember who you were and not what you did? It is awfully hard to recall that. You probably can recall what you were doing during a certain event. A picture may jog your memory as to what you were doing, but that is not what we are asking. Who were you being? During all those events can you answer that? Did you know who you were being? Does it now give you a different outlook of events this time around? Do you look at things differently? Satisfaction only comes in the knowing of who you are being. Do you know who *YOU* are? Satisfaction never comes to those who only know what it is they are doing. That is why they do, and they do, and they do, and they do, and they just aren't satisfied! Their souls are just never content. They say that they just don't get it because they are working their tails off, and they work, and they work, and they work, and they just don't understand it has nothing to do with the working end of it. They have no idea as to who they are being!

We ask again, who are you *being*? What takes you to the knowing of who you are being? The answer is different for everybody. What takes you to that knowing? Do you remind yourself, or does your higher self remind you by playing memory advocate? Is there inspiration in there somewhere? Are you or someone else sending you runners? It is your memory that recalls all that; it is all locked away in your memory. What is it that is going to wake you up? What is going to lead you to the memory of who you are? Once you have discovered the being in your life's existence, do you excel in the being? Who do you choose to be? Do you enjoy who it is you are being? Are you like most humans and aren't patient enough to get to the understanding of that question? Did you honestly believe you were just going to wake up one day and POOF you are now being? What kind of an experience would that afford you?

Are you one who needs a little or a lot, because that is what you will experience on your way to understanding who you are being. Remember that the expansion process is one of experiencing and understanding. Yes, it is a process. Are you putting limits on your doing that affect your being? Humans do a lot of that.

Have you sat down and asked yourself the question: *does what I do on a daily basis affect who it is I am being?* You will be surprised at the answer. Once you have an answer, begin to ask others. Most will not even know what you are talking about. You have just opened the door to communication that will bring in the river of knowledge that you have and can use at your disposal. It helps you become who you want to be. Can you see how it works? To know who one is being is finding true happiness and joy in one's life. When you are truly being who you really want to be, there is nothing else but happiness. Everything else is just an experience. It is something that you end up doing. Joy and happiness is truly who you are being. So, who are you being? That is always the question that one needs to get back to with all they do. All the answers in the universe are answered in that statement.

What is SOURCE doing? It is experiencing. What is it experiencing? It's being. All of SOURCE'S actions are its gainful experience of its being. SOURCE is in a constant awareness state of being. That's what it is doing. So, when someone asks you what are you doing? You can answer, *"I am experiencing my being. I experience myself; that's what I do. I am in a constant state of beingness."* Being is the biggest thing in your life you can do. Being is a constant state of consciousness. It is the same thing that SOURCE is doing.

If what you are doing is a creative expression of who it is you are being, then the process of doing works. But when you are just doing, and you have no idea of who it is you are being, the action is empty. SOURCE is doing in the ongoing creative process of being so that action is not empty. However, there is no satisfaction for those who are unconscious in their doing when their actions are empty. Everything you do should be a direct result of who you are being. Then it brings satisfaction. Then it is an extension of who you are, and not what you are doing. Are you being who and what you want to be? Are you in the never-ending flow of being who it is you want to be? Are you in the flow of thoughts or inspiration that lead you to those thoughts of who you want to be?   Think about that for a while.

Brad & Kasey Wallis | *Who You Are Being*

Nine ~
Where Does the Ego Fit in All of This?

What Do You Think the Ego Is, and Where Does It Fit in This Conversation?

Let's categorize some of the traits of the ego:

- Selfishness
- Prideful
- Superiority complex
- The act of thinking you need to separate yourself from another
- Doing things for self-gain and not for the betterment of others

A lot of descriptions and a lot of discussion went into writing this chapter. You can add your own descriptions if you would like.

Throughout history we have found that the greatest downfall to most human beings and civilizations is the ego! Is it just a three-dimensional experience? In other words, do only the beings that exist on this earthly realm experience ego? Here on this plane is where some subjects are without documented evidence as to whether a certain thing exists or not. It is just human speculation from one subject to another. Unless you have documented proof that ego exists on other planets or realms, we are going to believe it is only a three-dimensional human trait.

In the three-dimensional realm there is the illusion of separation. This is the actuality that creates the ego phenomenon and allows for the downfall of societies and, thus, the separation. If you understood the fact that you are no better than anyone else, you wouldn't separate yourself from others or feel that you are more powerful than someone else. That is the test, so-to-speak, of being human. There is an exception to every rule, however we have proof and evidence in this world that it is extremely hard to do this. Does a person live as a humble being to oppose the ego? And does being humble counteract egoism through demonstration? It takes a lot of discipline to be humble! When you are disciplined you throw ego out the door.

Now let's make another statement about someone's ego. A human being with an inflated ego is full of fear. They are always fearful that someone is better than them. They fear the outcome of an event in their lives. They are always in fear of something, so they feel the need to boost the ego to cover up the lack of something. Ego fits in the fear-based category of life. So how do you balance ego and humility—which is the opposite of ego—when you are trying to explain or show somebody something in your life's existence? Is that not a tough balancing act? Once again what you believe to be your truth is not someone else's truth. Through patience, understanding, compassion, and love, one needs to understand that the ego affects so many things in this life. It affects who you want to be, and what you are trying to do. It affects how you want to do something versus your agenda and the need to provide for others, even though they don't know, or can't understand what it is you are trying to provide to them.

Remember it is very important that one understands that his or her expanding and his or her enlightenment is not always warranted by the others that are here on this plane. Just because you are receiving abundance from your experience does not mean that others will feel the same way. Most likely they will feel the opposite of what it is you are so positive about.

Have you ever had a great teacher, or were you taught a specific principle in your life from someone who had a big ego? After a little while they became diminished in everything they did because their ego overcame who it was that they were. How did that ego influence you? Did you learn from it? What is it that you learned?

Now there is another side to all this: the lack of ego, or should we say the lack of self-confidence. Human beings need to have the confidence in themselves to be able to control all things in their lives. They must have control of themselves, and not others. Have you ever heard the term *"you need to take your ego out of the agenda?"* Where do you think that came from?

Ego needs to associate to a certain level of self-confidence. One can be an effective teacher and an effective student with a certain amount of ego. Humans can understand this. This is not beyond their reach.

The difference between the ego, the lack of self-confidence, and the gaining of self-confidence is a very tricky subject. There is nothing wrong with a self-confident person, but when self-confidence overrules or disallows self-expansion, then it is wrong. You then lose good judgment.

One needs to be confident in order to accomplish something. Without confidence you lack the ability to accomplish anything. An ego is a tool. A human being cannot be used by others. Your ego can be used to influence and teach. It can also be used to cause damage to other human beings. It is referred to as manipulation. That is why ego is so involved in this conversation. Ego is a human trait.

On other dimensional realms where energy intertwines with all energy, there is no illusion of separation. There is no fear of shortcoming for if you are connected to everything, then there is nothing you are without.

There is no place for ego; ego is a separateness issue. It is brought about by the imaginative mind that has created the illusion of separation in one's life, and therefore must be greater than another person. It is a state of mind due to the illusion that one must rise above another, that one must hold another down in order to gain, and that one must harm another in order to not be harmed. All these feelings and realities are brought about by that illusion of separation, for if you are not separated and are truly connected to all, then there would be no need to conquer one's self. Compassion, understanding, and giving would be the order of each day. To bring peace and understanding into one's every moment would be the agenda. What else would one choose to experience except complete cooperation with one's self? One would experience internal and external expansion through connection, and the connection to all other energy forces.

Through the powerful combination of energy, one's expansion is so enhanced that it becomes so immediate, so powerful, and so fulfilling that one's existence and experience would be complete.

If you can bypass the illusion of separation you truly free your soul. You allow your soul to freely connect, and therefore freely expand without the resistance of the ego, therefore you will expand your being.

Ten ~
How Many Experiences Do You Have in a Moment?

How Do They Affect Who You Are Being?

I began to ask myself this question one day: *How many experiences does one get or receive in any given moment?* I soon realized that this thought process would be affected by what you were doing or what you were experiencing at that given moment. So, I took my question to a higher knowledge than my own, and then I realized after my conversation with the entities that there are two different meanings to a moment.

First there is a measure of a moment in our illusionary measurement of time, and second, there is the eternal moment of now. The eternal moment of now is the only thing that is really going on in ultimate reality. When we say a moment, or someone else says a moment, it can be in different understandings, different contexts. The answer would be that in the eternal moment of now, all your experiences thus far combined would be what is going on. This would include previous lifetimes. If you choose to go into the depths of all truths it would also include the entire goings on of every other soul's experiences because we are all connected. In all possibility you could include not only the goings on of other people, but all beings everywhere because of the ultimate connection with your spirit to the all of SOURCE. That would bring your experiences into an infinite number, and that concept can be literally mind-blowing and hard to grasp. That can be a complicated answer, so let's simplify to just this earthly time frame and what this life's concerns are.

The measure of a moment in this life—the measurement of a time frame—can be broken down to the goings on when you are consciously experiencing something, what you experience when you are subconsciously experiencing something, and what you're experiencing when you are superconsciously experiencing something. There are all different types of experiences going on at the same time. Because your perspective is altered according to your conscious awareness, the question will then come down to: how do you become more focused to experience more experiences within each moment?

There are a lot of experiences going on in each moment, and it doesn't mean you are consciously aware of all that is going on, or that your focus is on each of those events. They can be registering with you in your consciousness in some form or another, and they can be affecting you.

The temperature affects you; the smell affects you, the colors affect you, the time of day or night affects you, and all those things can sway your perspective of a moment. Changing any elements in a moment can alter the experience of an event. The perspective of the previous moment will influence your next experience.

Let's say someone was just screaming at you and took you to an upsetting place emotionally. Would your focus be very clear? When you become disciplined enough, and you can bring yourself back into focus, or back to center, so that one will not allow another to influence or change your perspective and your experience. Are you creating your own experience, or are you reacting to another's experience? In every moment you're influenced by what is around you, and it affects the perception of your experience in the moment. There are a lot of things to break down before you can even realize how many experiences you are having at any given moment that affects you and your being.

It seems like such a simple question to ask yourself or ask another, and yet it is so complicated because of the answer one gives. The answer is based upon one's perception of the moment and who they are. One would think there is a set answer to the question, yet there is an answer based upon each person's reality of that moment. Does what you are doing at that moment reflect upon who you are being? We would say who you are being in that moment should reflect what you are doing.

There is an endless answer to this simple question; how many experiences do you experience in a moment? We, as humans, have no idea as to how that affects us and what we do. How many things can you count in a moment? There is an indefinite answer to those questions. Let's once again attempt to simplify with this question: How do I become more aware of all things within a moment? How do I increase my awareness in each new moment? It's simple. By becoming consciously aware of that fractional moment you are opening up your awareness to the moment.

Most people would say they aren't even aware of certain moments in their lives. *I'm not even sure of what I was looking at in the room. I don't remember if I was warm or I was cold. I don't know if I was angry or not. I don't even remember being focused in any shape or form.* Then how many moments do you waste, or how many moments are used? And how does that focus affect who you are and what you are doing. More importantly, how does it affect who you are being?

With focus and clarity, one can begin the discipline of living consciously in every moment with unbiased opinion based on the goings on of another being, or even the goings on of the previous moment. It is very difficult to not let what just happened to you affect you and who you are being.

How long does it take you to get out of this moment and get to the next? A week? A day? Hours? Minutes? Or just another moment?

There are plenty of opportunities for humans to experience anything they want; the universe delivers endless possibilities to you to grasp any experience at any moment. That possibility could collect on your soul and become the experience of your soul's destination not only in this life, but also in your ultimate experience. In truth, your soul collects all experience because ultimately your soul is connected to SOURCE, so you are connected to all things, and you can experience all things due to the connection process.

The universe is an endless cauldron, if you will, of all experience you could ever imagine. The universe has presented that to you at your time of birth. The universe says, *"Here you go! You have us at your disposal, and throughout your lifetime you can dip your ladle into the cauldron to taste any experience you choose in this life."* How much flavor can you taste in your ladle? Can you imagine all that you could add to your cauldron if you were told this at a young age? How much more would you understand? How much more would you dip that ladle back into the cauldron? Could you drink the whole cauldron in your lifetime?

We are here to remind you of the totality of yourself and the powerful beingness of SOURCE. At the utmost, we want to remind you that you are SOURCE, that you are infinite, and how infinite every opportunity is.

Do many people do that with their lives? NO! You may be surprised at how few times one dips that ladle back into the cauldron in order to gain a whole new experience. A lot of people will dip the ladle in and fill it all the way up, and then they just take sips of the same experience over and over, so they don't even finish that one scoop before their life's experience is gone. They just keep repeating the same exercise. Each time you dip the ladle into the cauldron it is a whole new possibility of experience. Do you take it all in in one shot and then go back for another? Are you constantly gaining a whole new fresh experience? Or is the cauldron too hot, and you don't want to burn yourself, so you just blow on it little by little while just taking little sips of it?

There are so many things that affect the tasting process! Your personality, your flavor for life, and your enthusiasm for life influence this experience to choose whether you dip the ladle again or not. Do you watch another being burn their tongue on the ladle so that you would rather let things cool down a bit before you dip it in? All this is in reference to the universe and having it at your disposal the minute you are born.

Speak to a newborn light being like this:

"Welcome you young, beautiful creature of SOURCE! Everything is at your disposal; just taste it!"

You have the choice of not dulling your taste buds in your life. Do your actions dull your taste buds? There are plenty of actions that do that! Depression dulls your experience, substance abuse dulls the experience, control dulls the experience, and the list can go on and on. You can break it down for any subject if you would like.

Many humans coast through life eating the same oatmeal and not even trying something else because it would change something. If that is what they have decided to do this time around, then they are only going to experience one form of flavor. But there are so many other forms of oatmeal out there!

Then there are those that take that piece of ginger and cleanse their palate in between each bite to gain a fresh experience from each flavor of each bite, and to not have anything residual from the previous bite influence their next taste. What is taking away from the flavor of your experience? Is there something that is happening or going on that is taking away from the new experience you are seeking? Is a previous experience clouding your new experience? Do you walk into the new experience pure? Are you cleansed from any residue of your past experience? Have you ever even thought of that? Does what you are doing affect who you are being?

Now here is the irony of it all: you decide to be born into a new life experience that is pure! You have cleansed yourself by being reborn in a new life experience! See any irony in any of this? You are reborn; it is a do over and a rebirth of experience.

Human beings have distorted the terminology to work to their advantage! Religions and forms of organizations have taken a simple, true concept and have turned it into one of control. You must be born again! They teach that you must be cleansed by fire, washed and anointed, all because you are an unclean being! No wonder we are all distorted by the illusion.

You are merely trying to make a clean experience for your life without having any previous experience, or should we say previous lifetimes, affect what it is you are doing. Isn't there a so-called oxy-moron situation being created here? Doesn't it affect everything? It sounds like a dementia experience doesn't it? Are you merely trying to hurry up the experience? Did a human being not gain enough experience in their conscious experience and not gain something in this life's existence? Are they hurrying up the process to gain more experience to get caught up? This is where the confusion comes in. Are you trying to make up lost time? Knowing that time is of no relevance, are you trying to gain some lost experience this time around, and the so-called experts believe you are out of it because they don't understand what you are doing?

There is always something going on pertaining to the agenda of the soul. When an event happens, it is an agenda that is being filled. For example, if someone gets brain cancer or dementia in his or her lifetime, it is part of an agenda. Other human beings cannot witness this and understand what it is that is going on! It is almost as if they don't respect the other souls agenda!

People who say they just can't let something happen because they don't believe that what is happening is right, don't understand that the other soul is experiencing what it is that they are here to experience! For example, when you choose in your life's existence to be connected to someone—a friend, a neighbor, a family member—or you choose to be connected to an object—a business, a home, a lifestyle, an animal—you have decided to let what it is they provide for you affect you in the decisions you make. Nothing exists by chance because all things are controlled by the goings on of either your conscious mind or your unconscious mind.

Your ignorance can throw you into what would be called wasteful perspective. In ultimate reality there is nothing that you do, experience, feel, or see that is wasted, but that is only in ultimate reality. The question is this: Do you bring your conscious mind into the receivership of what your soul is experiencing? You can heighten your percentage of receivership, and if you do you will not only get more out of this experience here this time, but you will also gain so much power that you will begin to understand how much power you have! You gain so much more perspective of what is going on in this world around you and your experience here, just through your perception and expanded awareness of your opportunities for experience. This is how the universe works; whatever you perceive you experience! That is just what is going on here on this earthly plane! You are experiencing exactly what your perception of your life is. So, what is influencing your perception?

Are you a shining, bright light of SOURCE? Do you live from this perspective: *I am going into this next moment as if I am a brand new child that has just been born, and I am going to grasp all that my conscious mind can.*

Can you stay centered and not let another's actions affect your perspective? Part of staying centered amidst distraction is creating in your next moment. To control, focus, and stay centered amidst a distraction. Gain new perspective in every moment. Did you grasp something out of the last moment that you didn't pay attention to in the previous moments? Can you see in that statement how your soul's experience of superconscious expansion, subconscious expansion, and conscious expansion contribute to your ongoing experience?

If you were sitting in a white room with no doors or windows, and there was just you and the whiteness of the room, how would you know who you are? If no one else is around to influence you, how do you know who you are? How do you begin to know you? Are you having the same experience as one who is somewhere else? How do you know if no one is there to tell you? Is the human who is in New York City amidst all the rushing of traffic and chaos experiencing the same thing you are in that white room? Of course, it is possible because it all comes down to conscious controlled experience. What you can imagine you will experience, which is exactly what is going on around you. There is a slowed down process here. There is a gravitational pull that slows things down here. Once your soul leaves this plane, everything happens so fast it happens during the process of the thought! When a contemplated thought is born you begin the experience.

If you can gain a conscious knowledge of this, not only does your perception and knowledge change, but it becomes sweeter. You can taste each savory ingredient that is in that ladle we talked about earlier. You can appreciate everything around you. The beauty in all little tiny things. The light on something you haven't noticed before. Or even how nice the blanket smells. It all seems so very simple, but it is all part of the human experience, which then resides upon your soul's experience of ultimate experience, and all that is collective and goes back to SOURCE.

Another great way of looking at it is that you are a runner sent out from SOURCE. Go out and gain as much experience as you can; you are on a treasure hunt for SOURCE and for experience. The one who brings me back the most experience wins the treasure. So how long is your scavenger hunt list? Is it four things long, or is it a billion things long? Are you going to collect everything you possibly can?

Just be aware of all the influences that are out there! The illusion of disconnection hits you the minute you enter this earthly plane, and you have decided to play a game with it. Because we don't get all the things on our list, time and time again, we do it over again. SOURCE allows us this game to play because it gains expansion every time you do.

How influenced do you become by the goings on around you? Do you spend lifetimes swimming in the pool around you? Do you spend your life's existence scrubbing a floor to gain the experience as some do? Do you understand that you have the power to control the experience gained from a single moment?

Are you beginning to understand that there is no set number for possibilities and experiences in this lifetime? It is as many as you could possibly imagine! Are you stuck in a pattern in your life? Do you know who you are being, or just what you are doing in this life?

Whether you gain one understanding or a billion, whether you have one experience or a trillion, whatever you choose to experience in this lifetime's existence is completely up to you.   Go out and experience and gain new understandings!

Eleven ~
Through Broad Expansion the Spirit and Soul Grow

Other beings that sit in other dimensions love to watch us as we play in this three-dimensional realm. Wouldn't it be nice to have an experience where we could switch places where they would be permitted to come into this realm, and we would be permitted to go to their realm at some point in our lifetime? How many sensitive and spiritually minded people would open their minds to such an experience?

Due to the communicative process that is now available, the experience of the news, and the information that is broadcast via satellite and world transmission, the mere suggestion of a phenomenon where we could communicate with other dimensional beings would send humans into the thought process of the occurrence. It could possibly put them into the contemplative thought of the process, so the awareness would start to rise. The creation of it would then begin.

Due to what we have coming in about this earthly time frame, as far as a lunar alignment and the lunar phenomenon, there will become an advancement of communication through devices. The word will be getting out farther than ever before to the mainstream news, and even the mainstream radio and Internet, which will stimulate the contemplative thought process on this matter. That will continue the wave of higher consciousness and awareness opportunities being provided by this alignment, but it will also allow human beings to have an out-of-body experience. Perhaps some of the other beings sitting in some of the other dimensions and realms will now have the opportunity to enter into that body temporarily and experience the three-dimensional realm, even if it is for a brief moment, per their request and per their agreement. They will be able to experience the three-dimensional realm just for a brief moment—in the moment of now—so there would be an exchange, possibly of spirit and soul, in the three-dimensional body. It could be brief, or it could hold the moment for a certain amount of time, but for that certain amount of time there is an exchange program. That is how you may have an out-of-body experience. You may have the opportunity to sit in the other dimensions and realms and get a grasp of the goings-on there.

Whatever expansive thought is in, is communicated, is interchangeable and interconnected; there is a sharing and exchanging process that goes on there. There will now be an agreement that will take place. The lunar alignment that has taken place at this time on this realm is why beings in the other realms have gladly participated in the upcoming alignment. They will be afforded the opportunity to experience this three-dimensional realm at someone else's request. Through their encouragement they are saying, *"Come and play in our realm so that we can come and play in yours."* Through broad expansion and through increased perception, the spirit grows, and the soul grows; the ever knowing and never-ending destination back to the knowing of itself as all things can be experienced.

Are humans able to consciously be aware and carry back to your conscious mind these events? That is the question. Do you choose to raise your frequency or current state of being so that your conscious mind is able to hold and house experiences that you gain as you exit your three-dimensional body? Capture a moment, re-enter it, and bring it to your conscious awareness. If you do so, your consciousness can't help but be expanded!

You can't help but raise your frequency and step up the ladder after this has occurred. It becomes part of your normal practice. Some have suggested that the lunar alignment is going to be just a temporary state. We would say that there is nothing permanent or temporary; there is only the eternal moment of now. If you can experience all that, doesn't it make sense to want to continually experience that in your life? Are we to believe that if you are allowed to experience something that you are going to want to stop experiencing it for the rest of your life? I don't think so! Contemplative thought holds your awareness.

Let's refer to the experience as a heightened awareness of self, or a heightened awareness of your beingness. You cannot go back once you have been awakened. Once you see it, once you feel it, once you are aware of it, and once you can do it, why in the world would you want to go back?

All this energy that is going to be aligned, will allow all of the beings to come into a heightened state of awareness of not only their own existence, but of their connectivity back to SOURCE. This includes all others who sit in between all the other dimensions, other worlds, and all the other realms and dimensions that exist. It is all in your choosing. If you think, and you contemplate, and you create likened energy, you can have any experience that you choose. This time, during the alignment, you will be in a heightened awareness and state of frequency; it is being allowed and allotted to you by all contributing and eagerly participating energy forms and energy beings.

What will you do with that experience? What would you choose to do with that experience? What does anyone do with a heightened state of awareness? What does anyone do with the information of the knowing where you are no longer believing, no longer giving into others' suggestions, and no longer giving into others' experiences passed down through time?

The internal process of knowing is the process of full connectivity. The process of remembering is now favorable for you in a more amplified state than it has been at any other time in this realm. Once you have had that light awareness, you can no longer go back into the darkness. The light will find its way through. It cannot help but illuminate the room. We would tell you to get yourself ready, even if you attempt to consciously refute it or turn away from it because you are afraid of the process or choose in to a state of fear, because illumination will envelope you. All others will be illuminated, and in their attempt to aid you in your process and in your self-awareness, you will be heightened, amplified, and magnified. You can't help but pick up on the residual effect of light, which is *enlightenment*. You can see the light; the light that will happen is your own light. It is your own awareness going deep within and seeing your own life. You are a light being. You will see your own light, so you do not need to falsify what you believe that you see.

Some beings will be able to see other light that is in the room, and they will be elated in that process! They will eagerly share that process with others, but if you cannot see the lights sitting in the room around someone else, the true question is - you can find your light that is within? That is the what is happening with the alignment, which are the goings-on at everyone's request.

Those that choose to find fear-based experience will find their experience of fear this time around no matter what the situation and no matter what the opportunity. There is little that can be done for those souls in the sense of awakening this time around. Rest assured they will be awakened in their time. For those who are sitting on the fence, this can be such an incredible re-birthing process of your own memory in connection, and others will gladly demonstrate to you the remembering process to your own awakening.

Textures will become more extreme. Colors will become more concentrated. Depths, tastes, smells, frequencies, vibrations will naturally become more intensified to anybody who is becoming a higher light energy being because those frequencies will readily match a higher state of frequency. The lower state of frequency, which is a frequency that hides things, hides things in the matter, hides things in the darkness of the matter, can be broken through. As we have spoken of before, people will become very, very sensitive to the energy that is around them. They will become very sensitive to the goings-on around them. They will sometimes feel the subject matter. They will sometimes feel victimized by the goings-on.

Oddly enough, the economic situation on this plane, has driven humans to become more aware of themselves, more aware of some of the simpler processes in life, more aware of the structure, and the way we have structured our societies and governments here on this plane. All of it is in the beautiful alignment of the opportunity for our frequencies to be raised.

What is the frequency of your beingness? What does that feel like? And what are the stages that one might experience in going back to their lightness, and going back to their beingness? How does that shift your consciousness, and how does it shift your experience? This is a time for the encouragement of others to join this process, and your encouragement to others for finding their knowing of their own beingness.

Are you reminded through conversation of the opportunities allotted to you that encourage you to continue your process? Are you prepared to exchange with others your teachings? Others are going to come along who are going to tell you their stories, and are you prepared in your knowingness to offer them your teachings as well?

Are you aware of other dimensional beings? Textural beings, oblong and symmetrical beings, gastric beings, and electricity beings. There are beings that exist in every level of the creative process! There are pure thought beings, there are contemplative thought beings, there are matter beings, there are form beings, and as you become aware in the state of remembrance of self by remembering the process of creativity, you will shift your beingness to a much broader version of who you are in this perfect moment of now.

You know this process. You have only temporarily separated yourself from the memory of this process. You have had to lower your frequency to such a low vibration in order to exist on this realm that you don't have access to those high-frequency memories, but they are in the core of your being.

Every single process you took yourself through to get to three-dimensional matter, you existed in all that time; you experienced in all those realms. You have been in contemplative thought, you are light, you have been gas, you have been positive and negative, you have been electricity itself! Everything that got structured on this realm you fused your spirit with it in order to bring it to life. You left a residue of spirit in it, on it, and through it in order for it to hold its substance and exist. Then you pulled away from it, and you went on to the next subject. You spread your spirit to all the objects on this realm. You have memories of everything that is on this realm that you created deep within your ultraconsciousness.

The flower, the plant, the tree, the rock or the river can regenerate itself, reproduce itself, and not only that, but re-create itself in a never-ending better version of itself because that is what spirit from SOURCE is, and that is the essence of SOURCE. It is never-ending, ever-expansive possibility. It is movement into infinity. Unfortunately, most humans feel like they can't go up to any organic matter and exchange or communicate with it because they are better than it!

Let's clarify what contemplative thought is since we have talked so much about it in this discussion. Contemplative thought is adding emotion to an idea; it is conjuring emotion that is a contemplative thought.

How many ways can you experience any one emotion? How much range is there in any possible emotion? We would tell you that as many light beings exist are how many possibilities exist. That is an infinite number! With each experience and opportunity for expansion, comes your depth of emotional shifts. You're not stuck in one emotion per light being; can you see now how that becomes an infinite number.

How many ways can you create different forms

of gastric organisms and temperatures and frequencies and positive and negative and electricity? How many forms of electricity are there? We would say more than you could experience on this realm. Everything that has been created has electricity through it. How much electricity can you measure through what the scientists believe is the dark matter? Science doesn't have the equipment to measure that, but if science can think of it, it is a possibility! It will be there to expand itself, and that is a good thing.

Even though there isn't an acceptance between the scientific mind and the spiritual realm, there is an acknowledgement that there is something holding everything together. Einstein's theory of relativity: Einstein knew that there was a way of measuring what was going on here, even though he was born and broadened by his pure scientific mind. He still had access to his soul, and that took him back to his connectivity. He even stated that there is more going on than the mind can comprehend, and more than the eye can see.

Human beings must remember that as they awaken to the knowledge of the knowing of something in their lifetime's existence, they must not take that information and just pass it on.

You must absorb the information. You have to experience the information. If you take it and just pass it on, then you have missed part of the cycle. You must also spend time practicing your own absorption of the reminding of your own knowing.

Humans are always very quick to just pass things on in their lives. But then there is a desire to always want more and more, and you just keep passing it along. There is time that needs to be spent in the absorption process.

The contemplated thought of the reality has been fed to you, adding new emotion to it and creating a new process from there.

Spend time thinking about what has been written of in this book. Take the time to contemplate and see how well you understand the principles that are being discussed here.

Share your ideas with others. That is all part of the healing that will go on inside you.

Twelve ~
Your Relationship with Life's Experiences

There are so many things in this life that need to be taught, and as a human being or a child or even as an adult, how do you find your core sense of self? How is it that you are happy with yourself no matter what is going on around you? In other words, how do you practice the art of staying centered amidst all the distractions that life has to offer you?

Beings need to find their center first and then practice staying centered amidst all the distraction. Not only do human beings become so emotionally distracted by the other things going on in their lives, but additionally, they also react to them and then experience the emotional backlash of the things that are going on around them. What is your perspective then? Do you hold your perspective according to the core center of yourself?

Too many times we find that once the children

of couples who get married at a very young age leave the house, the couple no longer find anything in common, and their relationship ends in a divorce. Finding one's core center self eliminates that type of experience in one's life because of the knowing of who you are. Once again, the cycle continues because the children don't know any different than what they have been raised with. That cycle continues, on and on from lifetime to lifetime. Everything in your life comes back to self-recognition of your core self.

Human beings as a whole are not taught that concept at a very early age. The reason they can't be taught that is because those who are doing the teaching don't know the very principle themselves. You can only lead and teach by example when you have a very complete sense of self. You've done your soul searching, and you finally found what your connection back to the SOURCE of all things is, so once you have done that, you then can show your children. Usually that doesn't come to you until later in your life by the time your children have already grown.

Sometimes in life it is the older parents that are much better teachers because they have been able to experience, learn, and understand things better. Then they are able to teach those who are seeking answers. Thank goodness we are not all being taught by grandparents or the older generations because that would be absolutely exhausting for them. Most older generations are looking for retirement, or should we say not being tired, all the time in their life.

Isn't it amazing that there are tribes in this world that still exist where the elders do all the teaching? There are still some primitive societies, even commune types of societies, where the young will give birth to the children, but it is the elders who will teach the children. The elders are the valuable ones in the society; they teach the children about core issues, how to be well, and how to heal themselves. Those societies live very harmoniously together. Doesn't it make one think or ask the question to one's self why is it that we, as a Western civilization or a so-called advanced society, haven't figured out how to even be familiar with ourselves or to keep ourselves centered with all the distractions that we have in society? If you are taught at a very young age that you are capable of becoming, or doing anything that you can imagine, or if you were in a relationship that allowed you the freedom to experience all that you feel you need to experience, how much farther along in your life, and how much farther along in your experience would you be?

If you have gotten to a point in your life where actions and understandings are different than how you feel inside, contrary to what you have been taught or what others are teaching, then you are awakening yourself to the knowing that there is something else better out there. Why would anyone want to bury himself or herself in the misconception that life, as it is, is all that there is? The fallacy that life as we know it as human beings cannot be better? Your internal knowing knows different. Your soul knows different.

Have you finally gotten to the point in your life where there is some self-discovery going on, and you are saying to yourself, wait just a minute? Has your soul finally started showing up? Are you starting to see things differently? Do things in your life seem to be different than how others see them? What is it that your soul is saying to you? Are you finally starting to acknowledge, or is your soul prompting you into knowing, self-recognition? What is it that is speaking to you from within?

In your human life's experience there is a definite difference between what you are telling somebody and what you are showing somebody. For example, an adult who drinks alcohol and drills into their children "do not drink," is going to have a hard time convincing those children not to drink. When you are drinking in front of them, or they see you drinking, that child is going to lose all respect for the adult that says treat others respectfully, and yet they don't do the same in their own life. That is teaching by example, and that is showing someone a difference. It all comes back to the old saying *"your actions speak for themselves."* Your actions are the only things that speak. Words are nothing in the eyes of a child. Words are nothing in the eyes of those who are seeking to be taught. They see something completely different than what they are being taught, thus the conflict in life.

The conflict between seeing and hearing and doing affects your being. By finding your own self, you find your connection back to SOURCE. Then your actions change. They automatically will change because of the knowing. In finding your soul, and self-discovery, and your connection back to SOURCE, you will naturally act in a particular manner. This is you becoming a much more connected person since you understand that all things are connected. Behavior follows the learning experience.

The art of allowing permits another the

freedom for self-discovery no matter how long it takes. They might get it soon in their life's experience, or they might get it later in life, but they will get it! That is the process in the art of allowing! The process comes more quickly. The art of allowing demonstrates to others the very thing that you are trying to show them. The human being who is centered amidst all distraction is practicing the art of allowing.

These principles are taught backward in the human life experience. So, we are saying to you WAKE UP! Let's begin the process of learning and healing yourself from within! Let's teach you the art of allowing, and how you, as a human being, can heal yourself by recognizing who you are and what your soul is saying to you. Wake up and learn the simple things that make life so fun. Learn why you are here on this earthly plane. Learn to trust yourself and your knowing. Learn to trust your spiritual experiences and the fact that your soul is speaking out to you. Wake up! Awaken yourself to the knowing and allow others the same courtesy! Awaken yourself to your beingness. Begin to do those things that allow you to practice that in your life's existence.

Thirteen ~ What Is Your Current State of Beingness?

This chapter will refer to *current* as three separate ideas in your beingness. Are you aware of these? First is current in respect to frequency current. What level or what frequency level are you in, in your beingness? Second is current as in the flow of energy that leads back to SOURCE. What part of the current are you? Third there is current as in the present state of now, and the eternal moment of now. What is your beingness? So, the question *"What is your current state of being?"* refers to three distinct ideas just like mind, body, and spirit. Or should we say, Father, son, and Holy Ghost? It touches all three sides. It is a portion of the tertiary state of enlightenment. What is your current state of beingness?

Whenever you are talking about your current state of beingness, your three sides, your conscious, your sub-conscious and your super-conscious, which current are you referring to? Are you talking about your frequency current? Are you talking about the river of the current of energy? Or are you talking about the current as your present state? The present state is conscious level. Superconsciousness is the flow of the river. Subconsciousness is your frequency rate. When you are thinking about something, are you thinking in your sub, super, or conscious state? Are you working all three sides of your present being? In other words, present (as if a gift) state, or in the gift of this moment, at all times. Then there is the depth for each one of them, and it is endless! Can you now begin to understand how confusing it becomes? Can you understand how humans get into a state of enlightenment? They are so far above everyone else? Then there are others who are in the depths of confusion? They spend their whole lives confused because of the current of understanding. We think they are problem children, or people that are uncivil in a world of civility!

We have teachers of this plane who deal with these types of humans, and sometimes their philosophy goes contrary to what society would like! Well, that's where the problem begins! We are comfortable living one way, and we have those that come here on this plane that can't seem to abide by what we feel is correct! Is there something wrong with the person that wants to run to the hills to get away from everyone to find their peace? Or for those who run to the hills who just want to feel the energy of the hills? Or for those who have spent a lifetime in deep meditation and understanding? Those who have had something happen to them as an experience can change their life or outlook on life. Where do they fit in to the current?

Problems arise when we have those that have gone somewhere and found peace, and they are going to pound into everyone else what it is they have found! That is a controlling issue; that is contrary to true enlightenment. True enlightenment understands the all-allowing process! The acceptance process! The tolerance process! They should be tolerable in the process just like SOURCE! Do you work inside the illusion? Are you working on your enlightening process? Or do you become caught in the illusion and get stuck in the process?

Most humans are missing the middle section of the playbook, and they don't get the three-dimensional steps in the process. There is a tertiary process going on in all levels of existence. They get stuck in one realm or another, or they understand two of the realms, or even a portion of the three realms, and they use it to their advantage because, no one teaches you in all three. Not just in all three, but in the three dimensions of each realm? That is the problem! No one teaches you in all realms, in all dimensions, or in all realms of each dimension. They believe that they can keep you confused enough to accept what is it they are teaching! As humans, you realize they can teach in between each realm, and in between each dimension, and they can teach you whatever it is you want to know because you are searching. No one is going to be responsible because it fits in between each dimension of each realm, thus the confusion. So, do you stay focused, or do you stay in alignment?

When you receive information do you understand that whatever it is you are receiving fits according to the condition you are in pertaining to the information you are receiving? For example, where were you when you got this information? What state of mind were you in when you got this information? Are you sharing this experience with others? Or is it just an individual experience? All these have different energy levels attached to them. How you felt at the time, where you were at, what you were doing, and was something else affecting or helping in the receivership of this energy? Can you see how all this affects what you are receiving and the flow, or current, of what you receive?

When you start recognizing these simple adjustments that affect everything you do, and you can analyze and understand where the information is coming from, and how you are receiving it, we can guarantee you will never look at, or receive, information again in the same way. That is enlightenment in its easiest and simplest form!

You are on your way to becoming an enlightened human being. You begin to understand things in the three-sided form of understanding. All understanding comes at you in those three ways. Which level are you receiving it at? Let me give you a quick example. You receive information of a certain inspiring nature, and it makes you feel a certain way. You then talk to someone else about what has happened to you, and how it makes you feel, or how you felt when you experienced it. That relaying of information is not going to give the person, or persons, you are talking to the same feeling as you have felt. That is because we, as humans, are all on different levels of understanding and of energy to begin with. Each receives information differently. But due to the collective energy of all who are involved in the receivership of the energy that is being relayed, it is received in a magnified experience. Depending upon what level of understanding you are at in your life's existence is the magnified level of understanding you will receive information. A single person's experience is never as strong as a group's experience due to the magnification process. Do you see that?

The more energy, the stronger the experience. It is that simple. So even if you relay the information to someone else, just the two of you in the process of relaying the information or telling your experience, not only receive higher energy experience, but the person you are talking to receives it in a higher frequency because of the magnification process of two. Two people two times the energy. So, you can imagine the experience with more people.

Now here is the kicker: Let's say it is just you and someone else in the equation. You receive, they receive, and together it is its own creative energy (that is the third element in the process). Together the two of you have created more energy by just going through the experience. Hopefully I haven't got you confused.

We all are in the practice of seeing things and understanding things differently in this lifetime. We all see things differently; that is just the makeup of things. We are human beings experiencing life. No two human experiences are the same.

As you understand the equation and how things work, you can then see how the equation works as far as experience and understanding goes.

The more you experience, the more energy you receive. The more you understand, the more you begin to gain in your understanding. When you add in other energy and add in the level at which you are receiving the energy, and multiply it all together, it is not hard to see how one can become confused and even appear out of their mind, due to the frequency of understanding. It becomes extremely confusing. Yet it is really simplistic.

Here are a couple questions to ask yourself: Do you look at things in your life three different ways? What level do you look at those things? What level are you receiving the energy flow from? What current are you in? All these questions and answers affect your beingness. You certainly do these things every minute of every day.

Change your way of looking at things and change your perspective. Ask yourself simple questions before you react or before you make a decision. You will be amazed at the outcome.

What is your current state of beingness?

Fourteen ~
Do You Find Joy in Every Moment?

What are you here to do? Well, you are here to find joy! People say, *"Well, yeah, that's fine, okay."* Do humans really understand the impact or the continual state of that emotion? Does the emotion of joy raise your consciousness and energy frequency?

There isn't a higher state of frequency, or current state of being, than the state of joy and bliss. You cannot get a higher frequency than that. That is the frequency that is SOURCE, and that lives within you. For most humans in their lifetime they will hit a state of bliss just a few times. You could ask someone what the most impactful and joyous points in their life were, and they will sometimes name them. That's how few of them humans experience. They will never have the response of being in a continual state of bliss. That answer alone tells you how infrequent your current hits its highest state this time around, or in any previous time, because you are the most advanced state of being right now! This is the most advanced you have ever been!

If you are following the order of continuum, you will grasp and grow with that concept—because it is hard to grasp the eternal moment of now. Humans love the concept of getting better. You are always progressing. Humans believe they will hit the peak at some point in their life existence, not understanding that it is all just a continuum.

At some point in your existence you will be the light teacher, or the bringer of information to others, or you may decide to exist on another plane of existence. You may be the bringer of inspirational energy. Some beings love or choose to exist in a state of inspiration. There is energy and a force of existence in a realm of inspiration. It's just like the beings that line up your circumstances for you. They are circumstantial beings. You have angelic beings, and you have all these different types of beings. They are all particles of SOURCE that exist, and because anything that exists is a particle of SOURCE, there is no separation between you and the humanoid and any type of inspirational thought that can bring together a contemplated thought. You can bring together light, then electricity, then matter, and then form in all existence. This is the only order of the creation.

Do you have a conscious state of awareness in your existence? Do you deny the knowing of the eternal existence in your life? Do you do that subconsciously or superconsciously? Are you consciously aware of the existence that you are experiencing? Is it ongoing in your existence? Are you on your way? Do you have a totality to the knowing of those things? Does a small instance lead you to the knowledge of that truth?

How many humans are on their way to the knowing? They all are! How many humans have the totality to all-knowing? Very few do, or you wouldn't be here! There is no need to relive in the realm of separation and illusion once you hit that peak in your life's existence. Eventually humans will get tired of living and playing on this low-energy realm. Even though it is exhilarating and fun, you will eventually ascend yourselves to a more inspirational status, if we can call it that. There isn't an up or down; there is just a higher frequency experience. Are you walking around with all the knowing on this realm?

There have been teachers that have been here before, and there are some here now. Humans tagged them and worshipped them incorrectly. Many of them are afraid to say anything to you because you have separated yourselves from them when all they were trying to do was demonstrate to you your own potential of who you are. Humans would crucify them! They know this based solely upon human history; human history continually repeats itself!

The Christian crusades already proved that when someone said or did anything contrary to the church. They were persecuted. All wars are based upon someone's belief in a religion. Humankind would go in and wipe out a whole society of people just because of their belief in something. How dare you go against the teachings! Look at how powerful religions have become. They are all involved politically in some form or another! Do you believe that any religion would let you come out and denounce their teachings and not persecute you? They know they might lose some of their followers if you did because what they have been teaching you all these years just might be incorrect. In the very least they will counterattack you for what you are saying. There might even be an uprising of people just so that they could get rid of you. Everyone would justify that because they would say that it is in the name of God, and you are being blasphemous in your teachings. That is how they would justify those actions.

The humanoid that reaches the ultimate state of knowing sometimes just decides to hold it within themselves because they also understand that eventually all will get to that level of understanding. They don't need to teach them. Some choose to teach because it brings them pleasure, and in the pleasure, they expand others. Not all do this and that is okay.

Eventually there will come a protective layer or a broadening of the understanding of the collection of people. It will not be so one-sided. The opposition would be the ones who would protect the teachers—from the teachers that you saw teaching very beginning steps to making changes in your life, to the teachers who teach higher energy principles in your life—remembering that you were a beginner at that point in your life, and you are now a much higher energy being somewhere in the realm of existence. Do you fit in the teachings knowing that you are a beginner or a higher light-energy being? Do you have a much broader knowledge and understanding than others? Where do you fit into this existence knowing that you have all control from the beginning understandings to the higher understandings? What is it that you recognize, and are you aware that you have control?

Since humans love to have everything drawn out for them so that they can practice something, they will eventually become great teachers at every level, in between, and beyond to the state that they are headed. Everyone and everything that you will encounter helps you continually expand the process. Your teachers are at the same level that you are, and at the same level of being that you are. Bless them and allow them their space and their success because hopefully there is another level of people who eventually reach you.

The question once again is: what level are you at? Are you at a higher level, or are you still in the beginning stages of learning? There is no right or wrong answer! There is no right or wrong concept to learning! Some here on this plane are just in a higher degree of learning and understanding; that's the process! Do you validate your own understanding? You might be surprised at how high your level of understanding actually is! Have you found a way, or are you trying to find a way, to shift and change your life? Does the process that you are in bring you joy in your life? Does it bring you joy in every moment? That is a wonderful state of awareness to be in!

Even though you might not be able to hold that

state of awareness all the time, since the illusion is still so grand, just having the knowing that that is your intention helps bring awareness and more frequency to the process of what it is you're trying to accomplish. You are striving to turn your moments into a constant state of joy and bliss. It will make you feel better, it will raise your conscious energy and frequency, and it will raise your goal, which is to stay in a continual state of joy and bliss. At times it feels like a false statement, and you say, *"Well I'm just going to pretend,"* or, *"What do you think you're doing anyway? This whole life is just pretend."* But do you dare say to yourself that you are standing in the state of illusion and not pretending? How do you find the continuous state of joy and the continual state of bliss?

Do you recognize that every action, every thought, every emotion, every intention, and every reaction helps you recognize the joyous state? In other words, did you take a moment and pause to thank the universe for the warm shower that you took this morning? Or the mere fact that there was even warm water in your bathroom? I'm sure at some point there has not been warm water there. Were there times when you didn't even have a shower to shower in? Did you thank the universe for the soap you used or the coffee that you drank this morning?

Did you absolutely recognize the simplicity of the fact that you had toilet paper to clean yourself with instead of a leaf or a twig? Or the fact that you were warm in your bed last night? Or that you were trying to stay awake to keep yourself from freezing through the night? Someone in their lifetime has experienced this, and some humans might currently be experiencing this. Are they happening to you? If you get back into the current state of now and existing, isn't it amazing how quickly and easily we forget those things because of the illusion that is around us?

Isn't it fabulous that you can get from one place to another with a mode of transportation that is faster than walking? Now isn't there a reason to find bliss in every moment of your life? Could you just sit in an empty moment to run through your day and all the abundance and simplicity that goes on in your life that you have granted yourself this time around? You could be in a simple state of not having those things. Surely you would still go to a place of happiness because you go to a place of joy by having them or doing them. Do you recognize those? Do you just fall into the illusion like so many other things that are involved in your life?

Chances are you don't even think of the fact that your conscious awareness and subconscious awareness fall into the illusion unless you come from this lifetime's experience. Would some of those people who have pulled themselves out of extreme poverty in this lifetime's existence go back to that? Or would they go to the gratification state? If you have all those basic needs this time around, would you go back? Can you even really have the comprehension of what it really feels like to have a big piece of meat sitting in front of you and you're starving? There are no utensils to eat it with. What are you going to use to eat it with? You would probably pick it up with your hands! You would probably just pick it up, bite into it, and eat it. So, for people to say, *"I don't think I can find a reason to find joy in every moment,"* then they certainly are not looking! You certainly are not looking to the exterior illusion. You can look to the illusion and find a state of bliss, but more than that you have lost your memory of going within and finding your eternal state of bliss.

Eventually your advancement will take you to the state where you don't even have to go to those types of collective thoughts or conscious thoughts to find bliss. You'll eventually just go within, you will find your eternal sweet spot, you will find what is your eternal state of bliss, and you will just tap into it. It has nothing to do with the solution! You don't have to take your mind, or your thought, or your vision to anything external of yourself to find your state of bliss. That is really where you are going! That is really where your soul is headed! It is to keep itself in the connection to the eternal fire that is SOURCE! That is bliss! That is what people are doing when they are in quiet meditation, or when they are sitting on the mountain, and no one can understand why they are just sitting on the Mountain! Isn't that boring? Don't they want to be doing things? We would ask how could bliss be boring?

Bliss is a marrying state of progression with your being! You can't force it! For someone who is absolutely miserable and asks, *"How do I get myself to an eternal state of bliss?"* and for the guru to come and say, *"Well you need to just sit in this particular position and take yourself into deep meditation for 15 hours a day."* You can sit in a workshop and practice that for two weeks. When you come out of that you are going to know how to find bliss! That person that they are talking to looks at them and says, *"That doesn't connect me!"* Your physical practice does not connect me! It is the eternal internal connection that connects you!

How do you remember? By internally connecting yourself. You will find your own process of being connected, and by doing that, you will not have to follow anybody else's practice. There will just be a marrying of eternal intentional time, and that's how you find your reconnection.

All we are really doing is reminding human beings of what they are doing, and in doing so, you need to find your being!

Practice gets you into the discipline of getting yourself back to that connection.

Who are you being? Who are you? Is what you are doing reminding you of who you are?

Find your eternal moment of being; find your eternal moment of bliss! Find out who it is that you are, and you will find who you are being! Most of all you will find SOURCE within you.

Fifteen ~

The Pool of Thought

Very few human beings understand that the pool of thought has color to it. First there was light. Thought is of the first dimension. As thought collects energy it then collects color. Colors, patterns, textures, and depths. These are all contained, or should we say collected, in the pool of thought. The rate at which it is dumped into the flow of the pool is the rate of your level of consciousness. Do you contribute to the flow unconsciously? Or do you contribute when you are conscious of how the process works, and you are conscious of every thought you are having? Does it add momentum to the energy process? What I am asking you is this: are you walking consciously or unconsciously, continually contributing with energetic energy, or are you bleeding consciously or subconsciously.

Are you aware of your conscious contributing thoughts at this very moment? What about your day-to-day unconscious contributing thoughts? Are you aware of the frequency of your thoughts? Now we are dealing with conscious, subconscious, and superconscious thought. All these thoughts are different types of objects, so to speak, running or existing through the river. They all regulate or affect the rate at which it gets back to SOURCE.

You see there is a never-ending cyclical energy exchange that is continually going on. As SOURCE is always contributing to the pool of thought, you are, and can be, accessing that never-ending possibility of inspiration, or you can be bleeding it unconsciously. SOURCE expands with your contribution of experiences, thoughts and perceptions, and SOURCE loves the opportunity to exchange with you. We want to encourage your conscious participation in all of this because in doing so, your enlightenment process is abundant.

Let's break down the thoughts for a minute. A superconscious thought might be the stone that is lying at the bottom of the river. A subconscious thought might be a heavy log that is floating along down the river. A conscious thought would be the bubble that is floating along without any concern. What type of thoughts are you having in your daily routine of existence? Is it a low frequency thought, or is it a high frequency thought? They all add to the contribution rate of the flow of knowledge going back to the SOURCE of knowledge that expands itself.

Have you ever seen flashes of light out of the corner of your eyes? Perhaps it was a shape or movement? These are different frequencies of existence or thoughts going on all around you. A thought has different frequencies to it, or we could say layers to it. When your thought goes into the river and it flows back to SOURCE, then the river returns back with new knowledge and understanding. That allows you to gain the understanding. It expands itself, thus increasing the frequency constantly. What a wonderful miracle!

If SOURCE had wanted itself to have a singular definition, it would have already killed itself because that would have allowed an end to its existence. Humans can only comprehend what goes on, on this earth ship. What about all the other contributing thoughts and ideas from all the other beings and thoughts from all the other galaxies that are out there? They are all dumping into the same pool of thoughts! You could spend all your existence just discovering yourself! Isn't that what you are doing? You literally are SOURCE discovering itself! Doesn't the illusion stimulate new thoughts? How about new possibilities and new ideas? How to do something or how to create something? I want to be this, or I want to be that! I want to do this, and I want to make that! Where do you think it all comes from? It is a manner of stimulation to form experience from because one idea sparks another! Do you look at things differently when you understand that? I guarantee you won't look at things the same again if you remember this. Your brain is able to access any part or frequency in the pool of thought. It is simply a question of the open mind. Will you be open to possibilities you cannot understand knowing that in doing so you allow yourself the opportunity to begin to understand them? Or do you only accept those ideas that go along with what you understand now. The closed-mindedness is dominant.

Look at all the contributing factors. Do you see how all the things contribute in different dimensions and yet still contribute to the ongoing actions in your life? When you can see all the different contributors to the sea of knowledge that is in your own backyard or in your own home you begin to see things differently. As your understanding and comprehension expands so it does with SOURCE. SOURCE is ever-changing and all-knowing. Do you know the continuance of SOURCE? Do you know the continuance of yourself? Do you have a basic understanding of the constancy of SOURCE? If you are always expanding, you are never finished with knowing yourself. SOURCE is never finished with knowing itself. It is open-ended. Every thought contributes to its expansion. Every thought! It wouldn't have a judgment against any thought, action, or deed because it is an action to the continuance of itself. It is a low vibrational ego based human that places judgment against itself or another that tries to place itself above anything else.

When you find your place in understanding and acceptance of the constancy of SOURCE, you become fully tolerable, and you are all allowing. That is a good place to aim for! Fully tolerable! That is a tough one because humans live in an intolerable society. Human society is based upon the fear of death, fear of control, and fear of everything. Humans are so fearful of some things they would kill another in fear of losing something. Would you rather exist knowing that you had fed another, or exist knowing another had died because you had kept them from eating? Death is just an illusion. It takes on a whole different appearance now doesn't it?

What is enlightenment? Tapping into the river of knowledge. Tapping into all the contributors that are contributing to the river. Getting a sense of the entire goings on of all the events around you. That is the beginning of the process of enlightenment. With the open mind, light then sheds itself upon you. That is the beginning of how to understand who it is you are being. Are you listening? Be quiet! Listen! There is energy to be heard! There are thoughts to be heard. It really is beautiful music once you understand how to hear the music. Once you can hear the sounds, and the textures, and the depths, it really is beautiful music.

Do not get frustrated with your process. Once you start advancing, the advancement is fast in the understanding and comprehension process. Humans tend to get frustrated at whatever it is they are doing, so slow down and listen.

You now know the answer to what it is you are doing here on this earthly plane! You now know what it is you are doing here!

You now know the answers to the question you have been asking your whole life! You now know!

You now have an answer to the questions that others who have limited knowledge on this subject can't seem to answer! You now have it!

Isn't it amazing? Doesn't it feel good to tap into yourself?

Some will be happy with how far they have come. Many will feel the pressure of all the knowledge. Others will want to go on, and they can.

There will be others who will doubt their existence, and they are the low-frequency beings we talk about because of the power of this illusion that we live in. This illusion affects us all.

The fun will be in watching others as you recognize them at the different stages of yourself. You need to take the time to do that. You will recognize the limited thoughts that still exist in the thoughts of another. That will show you how far you have come in your beingness.

Your own knowledge of your current beingness expands every time you tap into the river of collective knowledge. Do you find yourself dipping your feet into it? How soon do you want to feel it at your calves? Or at your knees? Soon you will want to be wading in it! Then you will not only want to go swimming in it, but also diving into the depths of it!

Remember it is not what you are doing, but

what you are being, and all things will affect who you are being here on this plane.

Sixteen ~
Your Memory and The Pool of Thought

Your memory is tapped into SOURCE, and SOURCE is every possibility of every thought in what is referred to as the pool of thought. When you have a thought, or when you have a thought in the three-dimensional realm, your brain works as a receiver to the pool of thought. Your brain is a three-dimensional part of your three-dimensional body and is a very slowed down version of energy. The pool of thought has all frequencies and all possibilities of thought in it, so it provides for all. It houses thoughts that all frequency beings have the opportunity to tap into.

One might presume that because we are three-dimensional beings (slowed down vibration), that we would be at a disadvantage when it comes to the thoughts, we are able to access because of our matter-based form, but that is a false impression. Your brain has the ability to access all thoughts in the universe; it just usually isn't fully activated.

When you leave this realm, you experience things instantaneously. There is no lack or lag in time with your thoughts. Once you don't have a three-dimensional brain to filter all of your thoughts, the absorption process is instantaneous. That's why when you leave this realm, you experience exactly what you are thinking about in the very moment you are thinking about it. That's why each humanoid experiences whatever their mind has created for them when they die or leave their body. They are going to experience exactly what they believe. Now if they choose to experience something that someone else has experienced, then yes, they will experience exactly what someone else has told them they will experience. They have given into someone else's teachings or ideas as to what is to follow you when you leave this realm. That is why a certain amount of people have the same experience because others have told them that this is the experience that they will go through. Once again that can be a suggestive idea for you to think about, and that's why you experience that experience. So, whose thoughts are you having? And what thought is yours? Can you see that there is a difference between them? Are you having an original thought? Are you going with your own knowing realizing that knowing is your experience, but believing somebody else's? Believing in something is taking somebody else's word for it; it is the process of getting to the knowing. Knowing is ownership of the information. You may know your own thoughts, or you may know someone else's, but which thoughts do you choose? We know that by going to the knowing within one's self and not relying on another's idea is true mastery or beingness. Your soul knows itself. It knows that it is a light being from SOURCE, and therefore it is SOURCE itself. But with time false teachings from others can become your belief and then turn into your knowing that gets recorded on your soul. It builds up and covers the light within, and the soul temporarily forgets its own self. Then you experience through reaction instead of creation. You have given your power away and will experience that which someone else suggests.

Once you access all possibility or all-knowing, there is a natural process that comes with the evolution of enlightenment. Once you understand that by hitting the full access point of the totality of knowing that all is well, everyone else then is allowed the same process. So, when a humanoid along this journey asks for help, and they ask for runners to come to them, and they may ask for the reminders to come to them to remind them to get to where they are going by practicing the law of allowing an enlightened being, it allows the lower frequency being their process. They will encourage the "going within" to access all answers.

Why do humans go to school? Why do humans look for answers? You are trying to expand yourselves and to experience. As you experience you expand SOURCE. Argumentatively you could say that you already know everything; it is just the remembering that you are doing here at this time in your life. We really don't learn anything new. All possibility already exists in the pool of thought; we just tap into the remembering of certain things. Those things will coincide with your frequency or your ability to accept the idea.

Your brain, being three-dimensional, can access memories that you have had in your life, and it processes and provides them for you. It's almost like the replaying of a tape recorder if you will. The memory gets thrown back up into the pool of thought, and you are merely re-tapping into the pool of thought, thus providing yourself with that experience. The human brain also houses a memory bank. Within that memory bank you access memories and replay them. However, one needs to remember that all of that memory is thrown into the pool of thought, thus providing you with memories of a past life. You wouldn't be tapping into your previous life's brain to have a previous life memory; you would be merely tapping into the pool of thought. Because your memory bank is tapped into the pool of thought, you are allowed to recall those memories. Let me give you an example. As a child you were playing with some friends, or even some of your family members, and there was an event that happened that you recall quite frequently throughout your life. Due to the fact that you are not allowed to tap into the other three-dimensional brains that are housed in each of those humans' bodies, how is it that they subsequently remember the same event? One would argue that they witnessed the event, so they can then remember that event. But what is the witnessing of the event? Is that not a memory? Everyone who witnessed the event or had a memory of the event is allowed by the three-dimensional brain to tap into that pool of thought and recall those events that they witnessed. The same is true in recalling past life experience. Your brain is allowed to recall past experiences, and for many humans they do. For those who don't it could be that they would spend so much of their time dwelling on their past life experience that they wouldn't be experiencing this life's experience. Perhaps it's just that they are not open to the possibility of doing it, so they would not experience it.

When a human being is hypnotized, they recall past life, or childhood, experiences through the hypnosis process. Your brain is tapped into the pool thought and allows you to recall those past events. It would have to be that way because how else could you have access to your brains in previous lives? You literally do not have another brain that you are tapping into; you are merely tapping into the pool of thought, and it is that pool of thought that carries all of those memories. Now, for the sake of argument, there are things that are housed in your brain that you use for your survival. For example, how would you feed yourself? How would you clothe yourself? The brain also helps the body function. The brain houses memory of this lifetime. It is your spirit that taps into the thought pool and creates things for you—new, old, or indifferent—by tapping into the pool of thought.

So, getting back to what we were originally talking about, you have a thought. Your thought then goes into what is called the pool of thought. Now let's take go just one step further. When you have a thought, since you are not really having a new thought, you are merely catching a glimpse of the light of that thought. You are then having what we would refer to as a new remembrance. Due to the fact that your thought is different than someone else's thought, your thought expands SOURCE, and someone else's thought expands SOURCE. You can see how the thought process expands the pool of thought. In other words, how you contemplate a thought, and how another contemplates a thought, even if it is the same thought, the thought is different. All thought expands SOURCE because no two people have the exact same perception of an idea, or event or possibility.

Then one could argue that all possibility exists in the pool of thought, and you are just merely catching a glimpse or a fragment of all possibility. If you have trained your mind enough, you could literally tap into other peoples' thoughts since they all exist in the pool of thought.

All possibility is going on. Theoretically, it is one way of explaining the process when you try to grasp the idea that all things are possible. Since there is still a filtering system that is going on in a three-dimensional body, you will never be able to understand or comprehend all possibilities.

Once you leave this three-dimensional realm, and you are away from the filtering system, and away from the slowed down process of the three-dimensional realm, you will re-member, and you will get back to the knowingness of all. Each time you try to explain something to someone on this realm there is a certain loss due to interpretation and lack of language. Through intention there is a percentage that is lost. Through interpretation there is percentage lost. It isn't until you separate yourself from this three-dimensional body, from your three-dimensional brain, and from your three-dimensional organs that all act as filtering systems so you can exist here on this realm that you then gain a total understanding and comprehension of all things.

Each time that a soul leaves SOURCE and steps into the three-dimensional realm, there is a filtering system that takes place to slow down the process, to slow down the understanding, and to slow down your comprehension. It is due to that slowing down process that you collect matter; in other words, things in your life begin to matter.

A bright spot to think about is that, due to the fact that you are here, you are here gaining more experience now than you were the last time. All the beings that exist here at this moment are getting a percentage of all of the knowing. That's why no two persons are exactly the same or have the same experience. It is continual possibility of self.

Seventeen ~ Reflection and Possibilities

We have talked about the pool of thought, how we are able to tap into it, and what its purpose is for our usage here on this earthly plane. Let's take that conversation one step further and ask you this question: what is your reflection in the pool of thought? Realize that a reflection in a mirror is an image that is the direct copy looking back at you. If you were to look into the pool of thought, the reflection would be a mirrored image looking back at you, and that reflection would be made up of somebody else's thoughts. Would you be open enough to see what somebody else is thinking and let your mind be open enough to see the direct reflection of somebody else's possibility?

When you look at something, do you see exactly what it is you are looking at and correlate that by looking into something in the pool of thought, or do you see through it? So, using the mirror as an example, by looking into the pool of thought you would be seeing what someone else is seeing at the time it goes into the pool. You could be seeing someone else's thoughts! And you are seeing their thoughts and not your own. You would get someone else's perspective and understanding about a certain thought. How important would that be to you?

The understanding and comprehension of the pool of thought is a huge understanding for the human brain to grasp. It is a huge remembering process. You would then realize that all possibilities are set within the realms of the pool of thought because everything that is possible or comes to be starts with a thought. Now can you see yourself in those thoughts? Can you see how you have constructed your own creative beingness from the pool of thought?

In past discussions we have talked about how other people's comments and discussions have created you, and how your identity is based on the thoughts of others. You become a reflection of the pool of thought based upon other people's thoughts of your beingness. Do you see a reflection of yourself off the pool of thought based upon your own perception of your endless possibilities in your creative beingness or by another being's ideas?

Most human beings live the reflective life. They are either a reflection of their own creative process on exactly what they think they are, or they give way to the reflection that is a distorted reflection of somebody else's ideas. Do you have a crisp, clear, endless mirror of yourself? Or do you have the carnival mirror that distorts your view of yourself based upon somebody else's tapping into the pool of thought?

The person that is doing their own tapping into the pool has an infinite knowing! Humans that give into everyone else's ideas and understandings have a distorted view of themselves. So, do you have a clear crisp vision? Does your vision take you beyond the illusion? Can you tangibly see the light that flows through the illusion and transcends itself back to all possibility?

Theoretically, if you were to place two mirrors across from each other the illusion would never end. The image would go on forever; it would be endless. There is only an image based upon as far as your eyes can see, but the image never ends! What, then, is your reflection in the pool of thought? Is it endless, or do you imagine an end to your beingness?

The pool of thought itself is a very deep level of understanding, and isn't it amazing how willing human beings are to give into the distortions? The minute somebody else suggests something, doubt creeps into your thought process. Instead of understanding and knowing that everyone will have their own level of perception, know that all possibilities exist!

You are only truly knowledgeable of your own opinion, or the opinions that expose your true knowingness. You know what suggestions are true for you and what ones are not by the way you feel about the suggestion. If the suggestion feels so good to you, it makes you smile, it makes you feel like that is the truth, then the instant that you heard it, you knew it!

Based upon the way something makes you feel, and upon the way certain suggestions made me feel, I remember another part of myself. That comment or that statement just doesn't ring true to me. We would then say to find your knowing, find what rings true to you right at this moment, and in your next moment you will be finding something else.

The illusion that we live in on this earthly

realm as, is very powerful. Light creatures, which are what we really are, did a very good job of creating the illusion; remember you are a light creature. The illusion is different for everybody because of your perception. The acknowledgment that the illusion exists holds the illusion in place, and your perception is your experience.

If we are talking about infinite possibilities, and it is holding you back from jumping into the pool of thought in your imagination, then imagine yourself sitting in front of the pool. Imagine you were sitting in front of the pond reflecting, and the reflection coming back at you is revealing all truth and all possibilities to you. Sometimes your own visions become blocked until things are revealed, or they are reflected back upon you with a reflection. It's like looking back on and experiencing things being revealed back to you from a different perspective. If you were to be reflective into the pool of thought, you would have a different perspective of the viewing of one's self rather than just in the experience, as the experience is ongoing.

A reflection is an opportunity to reprocess something from a different point of view. As you walk through your own experiences and your own possibilities, are you reflective of your moments as well? Not as in turning back the hands of time, not as in holding yourself back by clinging to a previous experience, but by stepping aside and taking a different perspective of the goings-on. Do you have a broader perspective?

What is the relevance of the events in the act of reflectiveness? Are you that broad-minded of a person? Once you have the information of being able to access the pool of thought, the first information that you received is knowing that there is a pool of thought, and that all thought exists at the same time! That concept alone is so broad to try to grasp. When you take in consideration all the possible thoughts from not only humans that exist on this three-dimensional plane, but all thought that could possibly be processed by any energy being that is able to create experience for itself, you can access that pool. How broad would that thought be? If you could try to tap into what a being living off of the three-dimensional realm thinks about, what would they think about? What would their day be like? What would their moment be like? What would they be thinking about? You can access all those possibilities. We would say that even if you don't believe that you have the answer to that question, your imagination is broad enough to take you to all possibilities. It is the broadest form of thought!

People believe they aren't able to play in the pool of thought. We would tell you to go ahead and play. Go play, and after you have played for a while, once you have splashed around, dove in, got yourself wet, and you've gotten out of the pool, you are able to reflect back at the fast currents that you were able to ride on, and the deep pools that you were able to swim in. Do you stand back and reflect on your own knowing of your own tapping in? Reflective processing is a broader step. It is the sidestepping of one's own perspective, and it is being able to step into broader perspective of the collective of not just another, but the possibility of all. That is SOURCE!

SOURCE is the broadest perspective of all events, and at the same time it is the absorption of all the goings-on. Once you have decided you have access into, and can tap into the pool of thought, you will remember that it is what you have been doing all along, and you just now have conscious awareness of it. Can you now take that awareness to how big and how deep the pool is? What is all pool of thought? What are all energy beings? What is all possibility when they contemplate themselves? When energy beings move through experience, do they then tap into the pool of thought? Don't they have to contemplate thought in order to grasp and experience? All energy beings grasp and experience the pool of thought. What do you think the tonality beings think about? Can you use your imagination to take your mind to what the tonality beings may be thinking about? Are you not a pure tonality being? Is it only a human that has the ability to think of such things?

Once you have grasped the concept of tapping into the pool of thought and the never-ending expansiveness of those possibilities and what it holds, does the human that is on this plane grasp the tonality beings' thoughts when they hear music? Why would that access be different than the thought of a regular three-dimensional being? Remembering that the three-dimensional being is a slowed down version of a being, thus being three-dimensional, they contain more matter. Are there different dimensions in the pool of thought?

In the totality of all the events going on, once you grasp the concept, you practice it, you get into the knowing of it, then you put your knowing into the action and the experience, then what happens? Don't you then receive wisdom? That wisdom is what you hold deep inside of you. You can access it at any time. You know this because you no longer need to have the experience; you just know it! You have absorbed it, you have created it, you have used it, you have used every aspect of it, and now you hold it as wisdom. Then you don't need to repeat it. That takes your experience into the reflectiveness or the reflection in the pool of thought.

Brad & Kasey Wallis | *Who You Are Being*

Eighteen ~ Are You a Doer or a Don't-Er?

Let's talk for just a minute about people who are doers in their lives and those who are don't-ers, or should we say someone who does, and someone who doesn't. There really is a big difference between the two.

Sometimes just telling someone that they are a doer or that somebody is a don't-er just isn't enough. Sometimes it's too hard for someone who is a don't-er to try to do. The funny thing is that those who always do really do all the time. They are always doing something. Are you working on being a human being or a human doing? How do you attach being a human being to your doing? Is it the icing on the cake of life if you can become aware of the human you are being and add that onto the layer of whether you are a human doing or a human not doing?

We could talk about it being positive and

negative, and we could talk about it being happy or sad, but you really could just categorize people in the two categories of those who do and those who don't. You're going to have extremes in those categories, and you can have laid-back people in those categories. You can break people down quickly, personality wise, in their achievements in their life and in the attempts in their life. There are those that attempt things, and there are those who just don't attempt at all.

Out of all the multitudes of attempts you are going to have, a certain percentage of them will be successes. Even when you fail, the people who are doers get the fact that by trying something, they are attempting to do something. Therefore, they always get something out of it. They use every opportunity as one of expansion. They always enjoy the experience of doing something new and different. They look upon challenges as something to work through, not something to run from.

Families can be broken down into those categories as well. Some individuals within families are doers; some individuals within the families are don't-ers. You might even have a whole family of doers, or you might even have a whole family of don't-ers. In the family of doers, they drive each other crazy because they are always trying to outdo each other. Now the ironic part is a lot of people that don't, tend to believe that they do. All they are really doing is attaching themselves to other doers because they are not accountable for their actions. They will use other individuals' achievements as their own.

So, are you an arduous doer? Or are you a selfish don't-er? How self-aware are you? Who do you blame for all your non-achievements in your life? Doers claim accountability even for their shortcomings. The doers will say, *"I was on my path to achieving this and I don't blame anybody else except myself for not achieving it."* A don't type person always has an excuse as to why they didn't achieve what it was they were striving for, and they always have somebody else to blame. Doers will always give others the accolades of their achievements; don't-ers only claim their own achievements at the expense of others. A don't-er will give credit to others when they fail, but they will claim whole credit for themselves when they achieve. A doer will claim credit for themselves and others and gives others their credit when they succeed. Can you see that they are total opposites?

If you break down each aspect in your life, you would soon see that at some point in your life you have been one or the other. There is always something to figure out in your life. There are always things you can look back at and say to yourself, *"I wish I would've done things differently. I wish I would have followed through with this or followed through with that."* The mere fact that you see and recognize that, means that you have turned the page into becoming a doer in your life. Sadly enough, doers always seem to want to help the don't-ers because doers always want to do for other people. The don't-ers will always be more than happy to let you do for them because they don't.

This is part of the dilemma and the paradox that goes on in our life's existence. The climb in life is to accept people and recognize who and what they are. It is also to realize that once you start your climb, you don't want to go back down to the don't.

Let's use another word instead of don't. Let's say you are disconnected. That would mean that you are no longer connected to the SOURCE of all things. For example, an electrical cord is plugged into an electrical outlet, thus creating electricity through the cord to supply what it is delivering at the end of its outlet. Without the cord being plugged into a source of electricity, there would be no source of electricity at the other end, and it would be disconnected.

When human beings become disconnected in their lives, and they lose connection to the SOURCE of all things, they soon find themselves in need of that energy. If you had full recollection of who you are, and you had full recollection of your connection to SOURCE and how powerful your being is, you couldn't help but do. You do because you know that's all there is to do. As a don't you are disconnected from the SOURCE of things. You have forgotten how powerful you are, you have stopped achieving things, you can't do it, you don't want to do it, and things in life are too hard. You have fallen off the recognition wagon of your own powerful self. So, connection is doing; disconnection is a don't. Then how does a don't become a do? Through self-awareness and reconnection to SOURCE. Then you realize there is nothing else but to do. There are no failures, there are no weaknesses, and in ultimate reality, once you get your mindset on that wagon, you are going to do. Now the difficulty in this is that the universe delivers everything that we request. So, for someone who is used to being a don't-er, because nothing ever works out, that is exactly what they get in their life because that is their request. Your experience is your request, so shift your request. Shift your experience. The universe will deliver.

Perception and experience affect your requests

from the universe. Your thoughts and perception are what affect you. The universe delivers it to you exactly the way you perceive your experience to be. That's why we don't hold onto past life experiences because they would influence our new life's experiences and our progression. Life would become way too complicated if we were to remember past life experiences. We have a hard-enough time with our own experiences now. You can choose to become anything that you choose at any moment that you choose it. What is the difference between being a do and being a don't? Fear and love!

It always comes down to the two categories of fear and love. Love is always a do; fear is always a don't. It is ultimate reality or illusion.

Ultimate reality is only love and doing because that is what SOURCE is doing. Disconnection is illusion and forgetting who you are living in the illusion around you. Everything in life, and everything in our existence, falls into those two categories. It can be broken down into different titles or different descriptions for different types of experiences, but you are still describing either fear or love. Connection or disconnection. You do, or you don't. Positive or negative. The yin and the yang.

It all has to do with acknowledgment of one's self. For example, how do you know yourself if you are in a white room with no doors, no windows, and no one to tell you what you look like? No one to tell you whether you are male or female, whether you have dark skin or light skin, whether you are tall or short, skinny or heavy, blue-eyed or brown-eyed? How do you know who you are if no one is there to tell you? How do you know anything if there is no form of contradiction going on? You have to be able to experience yourself. You have to be able to understand yourself. You must be comfortable with yourself. You have to be connected to yourself, which is exactly what is going on in the universe. It all gets back to connection and who are you being. Do you sense that you are connected to SOURCE? Or are you disconnected from that reality? Is there some form of approval that you need to seek in order to be connected? Do you feel like there is an initiation process in order to get into the club?

Isn't that a cool way to talk to your children and say to them, *"Are you doing, or do you don't?"* Can't you always tell when a child is a don't? And don't you want better for them? Let's work on getting you to be a better doer. Let's work on getting you more to the do side in life. When a child wants to do, or when you have a human being who wants to do, it is a very uplifting experience in one's life. What type of person would you have become if your parents or the person who had raised you had sat you down and said to you, *"I believe you are a doer." That is a wonderful thing to do in your life; I believe you will do much more with your life because of the fact that you are that way. Know that no matter what you do, you are doing!"* What a difference that would make in one's life, don't you think? What kind of self-empowering knowledge with connection would you have in all that you do? Would you look at things differently or understand things differently in your life just by doing instead of not doing? You choose to make that distinction in your life; no one else does. Only you do.

So, do you choose to be among the do, or the don't? Does it make more sense to hang with the do's, and reconnect in your life, or the don'ts?

As you journey through your life, and you come to the evergreen garden of the latter years of this life's experience, you learn things about your own self. Looking back on your own path of discovery, of the positive and the negative, and the fear and the love, and the doing and the not doing along the way, you make the decision as to what you would like to do next. More importantly, you decide who you are being while you do your next thing, which amplifies you as you do in life.

Brad & Kasey Wallis | *Who You Are Being*

Nineteen ~
Boredom and Getting Frustrated

As you progress in your life there comes a time when you are either frustrated with what is going on in your life, or you have become bored with what is going on in your life. Many human beings would believe that because you are bored with your life, you are now frustrated, but that is not the case at all. There is a huge difference between frustration and boredom.

When a human being becomes bored, they have lost direction in their life. They are unhappy with the direction they are going. Frustration is a stimulating emotion. The feeling of boredom is setting in. You will have gained everything you have set out to gain in this experience, so you are bored. You know what that feels like. You don't want to do that anymore. You have hit it from every angle, and you are beginning to develop a desire for another action. It's not just a desire for something, but a desire for something in particular, and that is telling you to move into a specific direction.

Don't misunderstand that being frustrated isn't moving fast enough in your life; it means that you are done with the experience. There's a difference between still wanting and experiencing and working your way through it. Know that you are still choosing what you get from your experience, and that is the driving force that is getting you to what you are doing. That is the difference between the driving force that is getting you to where you are going, and just saying, *"I'm done with that experience!"*

Just because you are frustrated that other people are not as fast as you are at doing things doesn't mean that you are done having your experience. When you are done with an experience, you have a satisfaction level that lets you know that you are done with that experience. You have gained everything there is to gain from that experience, you get bored, you're ready to move on, and you, as a human being, know your feelings best. To decipher whether you are done with something or not; one must be in communication with their own soul to understand that!

A lot of times frustration will move you to another action to help you get through the wall that you have just hit, whereas boredom is telling you that you are finished, you are done, and it is a finality. It's time to move out of an area, it's time to move out of the house you are living in, it's time to move out of the relationship you are in, and those are finality decisions one makes in their life.

There is still a certain amount of stimulation that is tied to the word frustration, but that is not true with the word boredom. You need to identify what is frustrating to you in your life. Are you frustrated with this person or that person, or the lack of something, or the slow progress of something? If so, you're going to push and you're going to find a way through it! Or has boredom finally said to you, *"You are ready to move on to something else! You are done with the whole experience!"*

In general, a lot of people feel both frustration and boredom in the process of becoming enlightened, and what they do with the awakening process is very stimulating because it is a process, but that frustration will set in because you don't feel like you are progressing fast enough to achieve what you want to achieve in your life. Rest assured, that it is just a process. You wouldn't be here on this Earth if you weren't intended to be here. What is it then that you still need to learn?

Human beings need to learn to identify their emotions. They do this sometimes out of their frustration. It is easier for humans to say *forget it I am done with it*, and yet that is merely an emotional reaction to frustration. Constantly struggling with yourself can be demanding. The totality of all experiences will include all emotions.

What is it this time that you are experiencing as far as emotions go? For instance, if you are in love, do you not experience frustration? How about sadness, joy, pain, or suffering? All these are emotional feelings. You go through the whole gamut of emotions hitting that experience from every angle. Ideally one would want to hit bliss and hold it from that experience. Then you will love it and absorb it, next you will hit boredom, and then you're ready to move onto your next experience.

Human beings have a hard time identifying their feelings. They get them so mixed up. There is a difference between anger and frustration, sadness and mourning, and boredom and stimulation. But if you cut an experience off without gaining the totality of it, you go back and complete the process at some point. One must remember that time is infinite. There may have been something that you stopped doing in a previous experience, and you cut it off. You may have attached anger to it, or you cut it off in frustration, and now you are picking it up in this life's existence. Can you see how you never run out of things to do?

Learning how to be in tune with your feelings is a tough task. Sometimes you need to acknowledge your feelings. You need to talk about them and move on to the next feeling. Not everything is a life-changing experience each time, and sometimes those experiences do change your life. There are times in your life where you know that it is just time to move on, and you are at peace with that. You have grabbed that experience from every angle, you loved it, you held it, your life has absorbed it, it is now part of your wisdom, and you don't need to do that again. You are joyful that you have had those feelings. Be grateful that you have experienced it and have it as a part of your wisdom; you should now be joyful moving into your next experience instead of feeling that just because you can't get it, it is time to move on to something else. There is a difference! Either way it is your choice, and some people just can't seem to get through that.

It is the feeling you are feeling; you just need to lay it down, get over it, and let go. It is a choice. But that's not working through your emotion of frustration. Your frustration is actually binding you; you get through so many emotions in your life, and then frustration makes you drop something. It is the emotion of frustration that is binding you. But awakened beings recognize this and are working on it in their life. They recognize the fact that, in order to heal themselves, they literally have to wake themselves up to the emotions that they have in their own life. Emotions are so powerful. In some human beings, emotions are amplified due to physical complications.

You need to remember that your perception is your experience. Are you one of those human beings that enjoy the extreme things in your life? Is it so influential that everything in your life has to be an extreme? Or are you a calm, passive soul that very few things in your life upset you? Do you recognize things on a smaller scale and realize that things just aren't quite as bad as you thought originally? Are you capable of recognizing your true perception?

Human beings' sensitivity levels grow with their awareness level. Sometimes people aren't as aware of themselves as they would like to be, and they don't experience anything until it hits an extreme level. They are not connected to the knowing of themselves; instantaneously that is the early phases of the emotional process. Now the emotions are the same, but the perception switches. If you are irritated or if you are experiencing full-blown anger because of something that has taken place, that affects your experience and your reaction. If you are merely frustrated because you're five minutes late, you can move yourself out of that frustration easier than if you are enraged. Your rational mind is just going to react.

So, are you creating? Or are you reacting? That is another way of finding out exactly how rational you are in recognizing your emotions. If you are reacting, you are off center. You have forgotten you have control of yourself. You don't always have control of what is going on, but if you are just reacting, you have allowed the illusion to control you. If you are on center, you are creating in every experience. If you are creating, it helps you to subside more of the fear-based reactive emotions that are in you because fear is disconnection. It's all part of the intricate inter-twining knowing of one's self, the connecting to your soul, the recognition of your emotions, and the appreciation of your range of emotions.

Emotions help you have communication with your soul. Emotions help you recognize yourself, and SOURCE, and all possibilities. Once you have a volatile reaction, you have knocked yourself off center because you have taken yourself to a fear-based reactive process instead of a love-based creative process.

Being done with something doesn't need to be a fear-based reaction; it can be a love-based reaction. It's a very complex answer, and that's why we always say, go within. Go with what your soul tells you from inside. See your light, let your light calm you, and let your light bring you back to center. Now what are you feeling? Why are you feeling this way? Are you feeling this way because it is coming from a creative basis? Are you feeling this way because you are reacting to something that is going on outside of you? It may just change your perception and experience. Just by calming yourself and centering yourself you go within. The final answer is to always go within and find connection with your soul. What is going on with your soul? What is your experience? What is your soul absorbing from this experience? What is your soul telling you? If you go within, and you listen, you won't be distracted by the illusion. Are you having this feeling because of the illusion?

Are you having this feeling because of the knowing of your soul?

Usually humans will feel a certain way for a long time before they finally get to the knowing that this is how they are feeling about something. That way it's not just a totally reactive feeling. It is time to move on, or it is time to move onto this experience. I've had the experience of desire. I've had the experience of acquisition. I'm now having the experience of absorption. I'm now having the experience of loving it, being blissful with it, and I am now done with it. It is time to move on. It is time to move on to the next experience. Desire, acquisition, absorption, bliss, and then moving on. These are the steps in the process.

A lot of people will just spend a huge amount of time in bliss, and they end up staying there. People have lived lifetimes in just one experience because they still find bliss in that experience, and there is nothing wrong with that. The continual state of bliss is really what the soul loves. When the bliss falls off and falls into what we refer to as the void, you're then done with that experience. But that experience was just so much fun! You've gotten the totality of it. You've gotten the wisdom from it. You had the experience, so you don't need to do it again.

You're holding it in wisdom. You can teach it through demonstration, you can help others with it, and it's now time to move onto the next experience. You may end up just having one experience that you grasp in one whole lifetime. Whatever process it takes to get every angle of it before you are done with it. It might even take several lifetimes, but you won't know when you are finished with the experience until the boredom sets in.

Boredom, we would say, is closer to a void of emotions. It's almost like there is nothingness. You can't bring something to you to help you react if you are bored with it. There is nothing there! It is truly a sense of being done because there is nothing there. You can ask yourself this question: what is the totality of my frustration? In many peoples' cases there are a lot of things that frustrate them. Physical limitations can become frustrating. You are limited to the goings-on inside of yourself. There are parameters to your limitations that amplify your frustration for everything. People face frustrating limitations in their personal lives. You might ask yourself the question: am I happy with what I am doing? If you can truly answer that, then you are well on your way to understanding what is frustrating you. You could quite possibly be working on patience in this life's existence?

Patience is probably one of the most difficult lessons to work on. Forgiveness and patience are two of the most difficult, and self-love is close as well. Humans have a hard time figuring out self-love—receiving it, housing it, holding it, understanding that it means treating yourself with love, and recognizing that you need to be loving to others.

Love means different things to different people; violence and anger, to some people, is love, control, and manipulation. It is all your perception. Sometimes your perception is based on your experience. We would say you would be better off if your experience was based upon your own perception.

It works like a pendulum that swings back and forth. If your perception is influenced by your experience, you're letting the previous experience influence the next. You had that experience before, and now your perception of this new experience is based upon your previous experience. You would immediately jump to a conclusion about the experience. Humans do that; it is the defense mechanism, it is a safety mechanism, and a lot of people do it out of fear.

Being defensive does not mean being fearful. Usually if you're on the offensive, you are doing it out of fear. If you are defensive, you are doing it out of love. At least you love yourself enough to not work in a damaging situation. There is a total difference between aggression and offense reactions. Sometimes you can just sidestep, and you have defended yourself. There are so many angles on any one emotion because it is also based upon your perception. What is your definition of any one of those emotions? Now multiply that with every soul that exists, and you can get an idea of what SOURCE is experiencing.

Boredom and frustration. Hopefully you can see them differently now in your life. Hopefully you recognize them as you feel them in what you are doing, and you can say to yourself that is not what I am really looking for in this situation.

There are so many ways for us as humans to wake up in our lives and become enlightened. By merely waking up, or should we say aware, it clarifies situations for us and helps us recognize so many of our emotions that have been buried all these years. It helps us to become better human beings at the task we have chosen to take and experience this time. in our life's existence.

Twenty ~
Potential and Possibility

At some point in your life you will come across these two words in your vocabulary: potential and possibility. You will wonder to yourself after reading about something, whether you have the potential to do that in your life, or even making it a possibility. Webster's definition for potential is: capable of being, but not yet in existence; having possibility; inherent ability for growth or development. The definition for possibility is: state of being possible; something that is possible; anything that is possible; potential for making something possible. When you read the definitions for each of these words, it is easy to see how confusing they can be. Sometimes human beings fail to realize that each word is no good without the other. Understanding that makes one a more powerful being.

Are you capable of understanding your desires and wants in your life? When your soul has reached its level of being, it will bring you to an overwhelming feeling of wanting to do something.

That is your soul communicating to you that it is time to move to another experience, and once again not having an opinion over the experience that you are wanting next. When you receive communication from your soul, you begin to experience. You are pulling and wanting without resistance. You no longer want to bury it or tuck it away. You move to the next experience more rapidly, allowing you the opportunity to more readily absorb the next experience.

Human beings have the potential for wanting more experiences. Human beings also have the possibilities of living those experiences. By referring to the definitions at the beginning of this chapter, can you see how potential and possibility can become part of your vocabulary in your everyday life? Once you as a human being understand the difference between the two—how potential and possibility effect the experiences you go through and the knowledge that you gain—it is easier to use the words in their proper use in your life's experience.

We have talked before about the wanting factor in the human life's existence. Don't confuse the word want in this subject because, as a human being, you should never go through your life wanting. Let's change that word to yearning. As a human being, you are yearning to do something else because you have absorbed all the experience from your previous experience. You have now become bored with this experience. You are yearning to move on to something else. You have had your experience from every angle. Your soul then communicates to you through your feelings—that's part of what feelings are for—the yearning or the desiring for another action that will bring you into a new experience. Some humans are very accepting of that process, and they will move immediately into the next experience because they recognize that their soul is ready for another experience.

Then there are those that are resistant to any change in their life. They are resistant to the communication of their soul. Their soul is communicating to them through their feelings of desire. Humans want to do something else, and experience something else, but humans will talk themselves out of it because they believe they have a responsibility to not do those things. They believe there is an agenda set up by somebody else, and that is what creates the internal conflict that can manifest itself into disease and disorder within one's life. Your soul is gaining experience from all angles. Remember, it is necessary to experience everything that an experience has to offer you before you will move on. When the soul is finished with experiencing what it is ready to finish, it will guide you into your next experience based upon what you feel you long for or desire to do next. Humans will argue with themselves about moving on to the next experience, and that causes conflict.

One needs to remember that, in the process of moving on to the next experience, this is just the first step of the process of this experience. You must also remember that you need to come up against this experience from all angles to completely experience it. Once you listen to your soul, you will be at peace with your soul, and then you understand the process. Human beings once again become confused because of their own agenda and requirements. Possibility and potential are always the start to the next new experience.

The mind and the soul can conflict at times. We haven't even put into the mix yet, what everyone else thinks, and their opinions about what they think. Let's say you are sitting in a specific experience in your life; you are extremely happy with it, and you are very happy with the part that SOURCE is experiencing. You suddenly start feeling completely done with that experience, you start to get bored, you seek change, and you are getting flashes of new ideas. What is it that your soul is choosing to experience next? Your soul can use your three-dimensional body to gain experience in this three-dimensional realm. There is an agreement that needs to be made between the body, the mind, and the soul. Potential and possibility are put into question when you start that new experience. Conflict sets in, and disease sets in, and the spirit starts to break down. Have you ever heard of the term a broken spirit? What it means is you are not listening to your soul.

There is an internal conflict or breakdown that is going on. Originally the agreement was for the soul to communicate with your mind and follow the soul's agenda through your experience. Humans have this conflict all the time, especially in a relationship. Relationships are always the first things that have problems when there is a shift in one's life. Whatever brought someone to the experience originally has run the gamut of that experience. Now you're ready to move on into the next experience. You may end up moving into a different situation.

Have you done this experience well this time? Have you made your *I am* statements concerning your relationship this time? Are you continually requesting to be paired to your match this time around? Have you chosen your agenda? Have you chosen your energy? Have you chosen to be in an extremely high state of existence? Have you chosen to attract yourself to those same high light energy experiences? Have you reached out to the runners and asked for the runners to be sent to you to allow you to experience everything that there is in your life? Have you asked for an exchange in abundance where things will come into the match and play? If you haven't, it is recommended to start now.

The difficulty comes in touching into new territory. You don't have any experience in the knowing of where to go. You don't know how to achieve it or how to make contact. You are learning the whole gamut while learning how to offer your gifts. You try to give to those humans understanding because there are those who don't understand. If you were starting a new business, for instance, how would you get new clients? How do you get into the knowing that things in your life are going to be okay? Once again, getting back to the potential of your business, and the possibility of your business, how do you accomplish anything? Usually it takes a few years, and a lot of stumbling, and a little bit of success to be what anyone would consider successful. This is no different in learning about the experiences of life. Are you going to end up being the master of accumulating those things in your life? It takes time to learn things, and human beings are very impatient when it comes to time.

Sometimes, for you to understand your potential or your possibilities, you need to say to yourself, let me show myself what I know. By doing that, you will teach others what you know, and that is all you can ask for. As you progress through life, there will be those who will offer you fake credentials that others will believe as true. You will give yourself the answer depending upon how you feel inside as to whether they are true or not. Humans need to depend upon themselves, no matter what, as to the validity of those credentials. You need to be confident in yourself.

There is no form of three-dimensional, linear-dimensional, left-brained education that can give you the gift that your soul can give you. Your mind is limited. Humans always ask for something that is attached to the mind's limitations; the mind will always be attached to limitations. Your soul's growth comes from ever-expanding possibility of spirituality. Do you teach others through demonstration? The longer you live in this three-dimensional world, and exist in this three-dimensional world, these conflicts will exist. Your potential and possibility, and your listening to your soul based upon your feelings all are a part of your current state of being. Do you understand what is your current state of being?

How in tune are you with your own beingness? How aware are you of the communication that your soul has with you? Are you open to the communication of your soul? One might ask what communication from your soul is. The answer to that is - it's your feelings! Your feelings are the way that your soul communicates with you. That's why your feelings are there. You absorb and experience by your feelings. The soul is emotionally driven.

If you go with your feelings without harming another along the way, you are then in sync with listening to your soul. In ultimate reality there is nothing wrong with that. There are others that would think that there is something absolutely wrong with that, and those individuals you will leave behind. They will argue with you that you should not be doing this to yourself because what you have done has hurt their feelings, but they are not in tune with their soul. They don't go with their gut feelings; they go with forced actions based upon other peoples' agendas and requirements. They move through this life with continual resistance from their own soul, and they are miserable! Their misery manifests disease, disorders, and distresses in their life, and they just can't see that. These human beings are the ones that do not bless others that are in their paths; they are the ones who need to always be in control. They have to control other people because they are giving in to the fear in their life.

We can assure you that in your life your soul will guide you to what is next, as long as you are in tune with your feelings. You get to choose whether you want to listen to your soul or resist your soul's teachings. Listen to your soul when you decide to make changes in your life. How do you feel then? How does something feel to you? The more you listen to your soul, the smoother the outcome will be in the ultimate experience. That is the difference between your current state of being, and your connectivity to your soul, spirit, and SOURCE. Understand that there is no opinion, no judgment, no requirement, and no agenda.

Your soul's journey is to move through experience, to own it, to love it, to embrace it, get it from every angle, and move on to the next experience. Hopefully it will gain bliss from every aspect of the absorption rate of that experience.

Whatever your opinion of bliss is at that moment is your opinion or your experience, and that will change along the way as well. The people that get left behind are left behind because they have empowered somebody else with their own possibility. They are not embracing their own expandability and never-ending, infinite possibilities of themselves. They have made somebody else responsible for their happiness.

Humans must realize that everything they do in their life is for experience. There are no failures! Failing is a fear-based experience that man uses in order to control another! You should ask yourself what you have learned from your experience. Everything in your life is a success. It either moves you away from something that doesn't work, which means you are being successful in your moving away, or it is moving you towards something else that is successful in your life.

Do you choose success in all of your experiences? At what point do you begin to see that something isn't working in your life, so you begin to move away from it? Change your point of view. Nothing is wasted. Sometimes it is extremely painful in the productivity process of becoming successful. How much have you learned? How much growth have you experienced? Have you learned what doesn't work for you? This is all part of the growing state! Have you ever looked at it that way before? Pay attention to what your soul is saying to you.

There are those humans that are out there that are experiencing disease, disorder, and dysfunction in their life, and they keep asking how they can get out of this suffering. How do you get connection? Pay attention to how you feel! Your soul is talking to you. Are you feeling excited in this moment that you are currently having? How do you feel about what you are currently doing? Are you excited? Are you enthusiastic? Then you are doing what you ought to be doing. Your soul is telling you. You are eagerly absorbing everything around you, you are eagerly retaining it, and you keep going, and keep going, and keep going.

Or have you hit a wall of resistance? Are you bored? You either need to move to another approach of your experience or move past your experience. You are full, and you have landed your agenda on that experience.

People will always say, well I can't change this, or I can't change that, or I can't change my job where will I work? Resistance has set in; resistance has set itself up in your life and in your thinking process.

Your mind is now fighting against your soul's agenda. This is resistance. What comes from resistance? Disorder and disease (mental, emotional and physical). Pay attention to what your soul is saying to you! Your soul will communicate to you. Make sure you are listening!

Are you excited in everything that you do? Sometimes you're content in what you're doing, and that's okay. You're still getting fresh ideas, you're still excited about things, and you're living in a world of contentment. You're still living in a current state of contentment.

For those who feel like they have a hole in their life that they can't fill up, need to change. Go ahead and make a move. What's holding you back? Your financial means should not be holding you back; you can achieve the same reality just by thinking differently. First, you could ask the universe for its help in achieving the financial means that is needed. You may be surprised at how that opportunity presents itself. Second, you can take your conscious mind, your conscious awareness, and your subconscious awareness and lock it into your imagination of what that experience would be like. You can feel it, and then you're literally having that experience. It is your focus, clarity of thought, and clarity of mind.

It goes back to the white room theory that we talked about earlier. You can take your mind anywhere you want. It's all up to you. Imagine what it feels like and imagine how it feels. Do you have a mental grasp of the details? You can expand and tap into the pool of thought to experience anything that you wish.

Rather than saying you always wanted to do something and never following through with it, experience it! Your mind can be your best friend, or it can be your worst enemy. It can work with the desires of your soul, it can help manifest something, and it can help create experiences for you, or it can talk you out of listening to your soul and what it is saying to you. Reflecting upon other peoples' experiences and tapping into the pool of thought offers you an endless supply of information and possibility. This is a reminder about the pool of thought, what it contains, and how you, as a human being, can tap into that pool.

Sometimes you can get more out of someone else's descriptive writings than experiencing the occurrence yourself. For example, how many times have you gone to the beach? How many times have you played in the ocean? How many times have you laid on the beach to get a tan? Then you read about someone else's experience of the first time they went to the beach. They wrote about what the sand feels like coming up through their toes, how abrasive the sand was, and how the sand softens when the water comes rushing in over their feet. They said they loved how the sand and water now feels against the skin. It is no longer abrasive, their heels are beginning to sink into the sand, and their calves are beginning to be pulled upon from the water. Then the sand hardens and dries on their shins, and they start to feel heavy. They are being pulled upon, and the water has a crisp bite to it. That washes onto their feet and they can feel a stinging sensation from how much salt is in the water. Each time the water washes upon them it gets easier for their body to accept it, and now their body is feeling as if it is being pulled into the ocean. The foam that is in the water has a distinct smell to it. How many of those things did you think about when you are walking on the beach? Somebody who has mastered descriptive writing can literally take you to another experience, and they can actually expand your experience for you. So, does it ever really matter that you walked on the beach if the other person can take you there? They just took you there, without you ever being there, and you got everything out of it. Do you see how that works?

There are different ways to take yourself to places to experience things for yourself. We are teaching you how to experience instead of just sitting and feeling deprived of an experience. Just because you have not physically experienced something does not mean that you cannot experience it; there are other ways of experiencing things. Now it is wonderful if you can experience the physical experience, but if you can't, this is one means of experiencing something. That is how powerful your mind is.

How about the person that has read someone else's experience, and they are let down when they experience the occurrence themselves? Maybe their senses weren't as fine-tuned as the other persons are. You may not be as enthusiastic about your experience, or you may not really be looking forward to your experience. It is once again your perspective and perception that create your experience.

Your current state of being will also affect your experience. Your soul relies on feelings. Your soul houses feelings that house experience. If you want to remember something about this life, attach an extreme emotion to the experience, and your soul will hold onto it.

Potential and possibility. Can you see those words differently now in your life's existence? Can you use those words differently now? Try them. You might have fun with them.

Unlimited potential and unlimited possibilities: that is what you are looking and asking for. That is what all human beings are looking and asking for.

Twenty-One ~ Things That Affect You Emotionally

Have you ever asked yourself why certain things affect you emotionally? Most things that are joyous register in the memory bank of your soul. You carry that from lifetime to lifetime. Many human beings are so concerned about their past lives, but we would ask you why you are worried about the past when you can't even deal with the now? In your past lives you were less of what you are now! Each life is a progressive state of your conscious awareness to your connection back to SOURCE! It is a journey of reconnecting yourself to joy! Every time you come back to this plane it is because you have not experienced pure state of joy continuously, which is the is-ness that is SOURCE!

The key is to find joy in everything you do and everything you are being. Humans are doing what is joyous to them or they wouldn't be doing it! Some humans find misery to be very joyous. So, misery must be joyous because, to some, they continually go back there! It is their choice, so they must be happy there!

You do not experience anything you do not choose! Anything! It is all about perspective, choice, and connection! That is all that this life is about. The experience you are experiencing this time around is different from your past experiences, or you wouldn't be having it! You do not repeat your experiences. You are only back on this plane to gain a new experience. You might be having what one might perceive as a similar experience as before, but this time your perspective changes, and it will create a new experience.

Your soul's journey is to experience joy! It has descended itself down onto the plane of demonstration to experience a part of SOURCE that is matter. That's it! Now the complication comes from not remembering your connection and previous joyous state.

If you could hold on to the fact that you are GOD, and you are the GODNESS that exists in every single moment you are experiencing, would it change your moment? Humans become defensive to that statement because they do not want to be responsible for themselves, their experiences, or their actions. Humans love to be the victim! Victim comes with the illusion of disconnection that is not good or bad; it is just an is-ness of experience.

Some things are manifested, and some are not. It should not change your experience of something. In other words, if you choose to experience what it feels like to be a king, you may experience that any time that you choose. You can conjure up that feeling. You can conjure up that emotion. You can conjure up that experience without having a palace to live in. Now sometimes it is manifested, and you will have the totality of the illusionary experience to go along with your emotional experience. You do not need the illusion to have your experience the farther along you get on your journey. Maybe you have been something before and it was a distraction. Wherever you are right this moment, we can guarantee it is a progression in your superconscious is-ness awareness.

If you want to experience anything, simply choose to experience it. You can conjure up an emotion! What emotion do you believe would be attached to any given experience? What would it be like to walk on the white sands in France? What would that feel like?

Humans get so caught up in the illusion on this plane that they can't grasp what is truly important here. Many humans are so concerned about the financial part of this world. Once you understand that it is just illusion, and you can manifest anything you need, then the financial part will no longer be relevant. It's okay to choose the illusion, because no one can tell you what you want to experience here at this time. What we are saying is that in the complete picture of the is-ness of all there is, you are able to create anything you choose. You can manifest things for yourself. You can say to the universe, *"In all my is-ness, I choose to be stress free financially in this illusion."* You can make things work for you that way. The difference is not to get caught up in your wanting the things in the illusion around you because they are a distraction. There is a variance between wanting and needing and choosing. It doesn't mean you can't strive for things in your life. The key is whether you are holding off experiencing joy until you reach something. Are you waiting until you gain something? Are you waiting to acquire something? Do you do that subconsciously?

Most people ask what their destiny is here on this plane? What is their soul's journey? We would say your journey is to experience joy and happiness. Your journey is to live! That is all you are doing!

Your destination is to remember that you are GOD! In order to do that you must experience a continual state of bliss because that is the is-ness of SOURCE. SOURCE is in a continual state of bliss because it recognizes itself; it is always expanding itself, and it does not limit itself. When you reach that point as human beings, you will no longer come back to this realm, and you will experience other realms. That will also remind you of those things.

Some humans have come here over 20,000 times. Some have only been here once or twice. It's all about the journey of getting to a continual state of bliss. What does that mean for you? Bliss means different things to different people. We would tell you that whatever you are doing is an attempt to be happy. That's what you are doing. You are trying to get to a state of bliss. That is registered deep in your soul's consciousness because it remembers it is SOURCE, and SOURCE is in a continual state of bliss. Once you have descended onto this realm you get so caught up in the illusion that you have become separated due to competitiveness, control, the feeling of lack and of need. You disconnected yourself from SOURCE because SOURCE is not any of those things. Humans are. Your soul knows you are on a path to a pure state of bliss, which is the GODNESS that you are. Humans unconsciously do things that make them happy. Now happy is a perspective. What your opinion or perspective is of the continual state of bliss is your opinion, and it is not going to be the same for the other person who is out there. That is how it all works. That is the expansiveness of SOURCE. Whatever you are experiencing, you are doing it because it makes you happy, or you wouldn't be doing it! You wouldn't be having that experience!

There is a difference between doing and experiencing. Hopefully what you are doing is bringing your experience to you. Now remember SOURCE has no complaints about what makes you happy. So, go do whatever you feel is bringing you happiness because it is expanding SOURCE.

If you are miserable in everything in your life, then you cannot do this, or you cannot do that. Misery makes a lot of people happy, and it's only humans who feel that something is right or wrong. That is an opinion. It is all about working your way to the state of bliss. So why are humans so consumed with past life experiences when they can't even master the state of now? Why are you in such a hurry to get to the next lifetime when you can't master this moment? It is because you believe that this moment is less than it is, and that you may have been something grander before, but you are your grandest version right now. Believe me, if your previous self could see how far you have come to the now, you would be impressed. You truly should not even be concerned about what it was you did yesterday! Your identifying state should always be in adjustment. Humans are only concerned about what will identify them. You ought to always be in a constant state of ascension. You should not be the same person you were a moment ago. You should be better than you were a moment ago. Then you will be better in the next moment. Holding on to what you did yesterday holds you back because it identifies you. Regrets bind you. Guilt binds you. It holds you back to a previous state of experience. Go to virgin territory to discover and expand yourself; don't live in a previous state.

Are you one of those humans that when you sleep at night you only dream of your failures in life? You just weren't good enough. You just didn't do something to someone else's standards? Are you haunted in your dreams about them? Somewhere in your current state of being that experience is still identifying you.

You can have a parallel life experience in your dream state. You can time travel. You are time traveling into parallel existences. You can get a glimpse of this, and you can get a glimpse of that. You can see that sometimes, when there is something that you haven't worked yourself through, things reappear through your parallel lives with very little variation as to what is going on. You could be in the same state that you are now in a parallel life. Once you move past that state to a pure identification of bliss in this life, you will no longer need to tap into the low frequency experience going on in any other plane. You don't need to beat yourself up about that because a lot of that is your subconsciousness. It is very difficult for you to tap into. given all the tasks that are at hand.

Your brain is designed to house all experiences and has the capacity to remember everything. Your brain has the capacity to tap into the current pool of thought without limitations. With the capacity that your brain has—there is so much going on in the brain—that you will not be able to have an explanation for everything in this current state of existence because of the low frequency current that you hold by being human.

You will not get all that until you have moved on, out of this existence and onto another plane. It is a different frequency of experience when you have left the human experience behind. There are very few humans walking on this low frequency existence that can use their whole brain. If you were to use your whole brain, there would be so many different types of firings going on inside your brain you would always be confused. So, when you dream, you are merely catching fragments of existences. Not all existences are the same as they are here on this plane. That's why peoples' dreams seem so odd to them. Your dreams are fragmented existence. If you were going to live in the totality of the conscious over there, you would be there. It is all just a reminder to you as to the goings on around you. This is all a game. This is all an illusion. You are always sending reminders to yourself of what is really going on.

There are some people who are so deeply rooted in the illusion here on this plane that they don't dream! They don't have an expansive molecule in their experience. They are so steadfast in the illusion that is around them that they are shut off from the messages from their own self as to the game that is being played out. When you are done with this experience you will leave. That is the end of that explanation. When you are done with this experience, your soul will leave. It may do it in all different types of ways because along that path, you are gaining some experience. Humans do not leave until their soul chooses to leave, and if you decide to play on this realm again, you will. This realm is fun to your soul; it is fun! Look at all the possibility of experience that is here. Look at all the variations without judgment of right or wrong. This worldly plane is just a huge playground.

What are you here for on this earth? We are here to live and experience. End of story! You don't have to have a certain job. You don't have to have a certain profession. You don't have to fulfill any agenda other than the thought that you hold. In other words, you live the experience that you choose to experience having come from SOURCE. End of story. Why do humans make it so hard? The human experience plays into the illusion. Do you think your soul cares what kind of automobile you drive? The human experience and the soul's experience are different. Human experience is anything that binds you. That keeps you from the totality of the pure state of bliss. Humans are all here to experience and live. Are you undergoing a new experience? Are you experiencing a new level of experience? You never duplicate your experiences. Are you progressing or gaining something? Are you learning more and more how to hold onto a state of happiness in every moment? Does that change your perspective of your moments? Does it change your awareness of your moments? Be happy in your moments. There is something out of every experience that you are doing that makes you happy, otherwise you wouldn't be doing it. If you can't see that, then reevaluate what your version of happiness is.

One of the big problems with humans is that they wait for something to unfold before they decide to have an experience. They wait and wait and wait, and they get depressed because a circumstance is not unfolding in the way that they believe it should. They are holding up their experience based on an illusionary realm. Are you one of those types that says to themselves, *"If only I would get this job, then I would be happy?"* Have you ever felt that way about something? Have you ever made that type of comment before in your mind? Why, when things are good, do you forget the problems that are always out there? Is what you are doing affecting your experience? How can you be so close at one point and so far, away the next? Do the moments start passing you by?

Humans need to find bliss in every moment. That is what you are working toward. Know that you are the totality of the is-ness of now. You have forgotten that truth in the entire goings on around you.

Humans rely on other peoples' information. Do you choose to go within and find your own truth? Can you find bliss at any moment? The closer you find yourself to bliss you will find your GODNESS. That's what you are doing here on this plane.

Remember the learning experiences in your life's existence. Emotions play the role of reminding you of that. Your emotions are trying to lead you toward happiness and joy. You have found joy when you become fully aware of every moment. So, add to your moments and enjoy.

Brad & Kasey Wallis | *Who You Are Being*

Twenty-Two ~ What Affects Your Experiences in Any Given Moment?

We have talked about all the experiences you experience in a given moment, and how we can recognize the moments, but what is it that really affects your ability to recognize and change who you are or what you are doing? Certainly, the way you are raised has a lot to do with things such as whether you come from a single parent family or a two-parent family, or if your family was well off financially or a financially strapped family. Your religious upbringing would have an effect on you, don't you think? What type of life are you living? Are you married or have a partner in life? There are so many different situations that affect us daily that it can be overwhelming. Now what is your perception of any given moment? Is it not your perception that affects everything?

By changing your perspective, you change your experience. By simply looking at things differently, you see it in a totally different way. This, in turn, affects what you are doing and your being. Your perspective or perception is different from everyone else's.

Human beings are always looking to lay the fault on someone else other than himself or herself. Humans have really given their power away. Victims always give their power away. Human beings are always victims of something. Are you focused on the unhappiness of the moment? You only gain more and more sadness the more you focus on the unhappiness. One who is in despair has given their power away to others, and they become a desperate person. You miss the possibility of the next moment.

Human beings need to try to see if they can grasp one more experience out of the moments in their lives. Just try to grasp that simple task. See if you can get a new experience out of your regular daily moments. See if you can raise your consciousness to become aware of the moments in your life, and then recognize a new experience in those moments.

Can you gain a new perspective of anything? When was the last time you started noticing something else in the moment? Do you start noticing something else that you haven't seen before? For example, do you begin to see the colors of a plant you have walked by daily and now the colors are speaking something to you? How long has the plant been there, and you never looked at it that way before? You can now see the colors, the textures, and how it grows. It is simple, but it is effective. You have just changed a perspective in your life. Somebody smiled at you today, and you know that was so nice. You were thinking about all the bills you have to pay, and what you were going to wear to work tomorrow, and the person who walked by you and shot you this little smile, and you thought: *"Wow! Did I send myself that person today? Did someone else send them? My guardian angels sent me a little gift today, and it changed the moment for me."* Did you not even notice the person and just continued on in the moment thinking about your worries?

What did you miss? Are you even consciously aware of the moments you miss?

Some people go from moment to moment and are not even aware of their feelings in that moment. Are you feeling hot? Cold? Achy? Confused? All of these affect the moment. Are you even conscious from moment to moment? Not everybody is! Just try for a few minutes a day to become more aware of your moments. See how things change for you. You will start to be amazed at how you not only are aware of the moments, but how you can change the moments. I can guarantee you that if you do that a couple times a day you will become more aware of the moments around you. You will recognize how many moments you missed before in your life. This is another form of practice in walking awake. Stay centered.

How many moments are there in a day? How many moments are you conscious compared to being unconscious? We are only talking about a moment. We are not talking about an hour, or a day, but just a single moment! A moment that you can harness and control for just yourself! This is an opportunity for you to practice controlling your experience by changing your perspective!

You can think of something happy for just a moment, and it will change your perspective for your next moment. Or you could think of something sad, and it will change your perspective of the next moment. Isn't it strange that two people in the same room have differing opinions or experiences of the exact same moment? Something can happen in the room, and both of you will have differing perspectives of what happened.

Once you have accomplished the recognition part of the moment, it is as if you have the ability to make time stand still. Or you could speed time up just by becoming conscious in the illusion of time.

Some days it feels like time is just creeping by, but the moment you are engaged in something the moment goes by very quickly. So, do you have the ability to control time? Actually, you do! You definitely have the ability to control your perception of time! Perception is what you experience. Can you tell me you have never experienced time standing still?

How about time going by quickly, or time crawling by? It's all in your perspective or your experience! You can slow things down, or you can speed things up!

It is a continual practice of becoming engaged by becoming aware of your power. You can totally control what you experience. When you get caught in somebody else's experience, you have given your power away.

How many experiences can you have in each moment? As many as you choose. Take two moments in any given day—just two times a day—and add an experience for yourself into it. It can be an emotion, it can be a feeling, and you can suddenly see something different in the room. Just add one more number to the experience of the moment for yourself, and you will begin to see how the universe works, and how you really do control everything that is going on. It's actually a pretty powerful exercise. It is an exercise in consciousness and awareness. You don't always have to be in a conscious meditative state to raise your consciousness. There are other ways of actively raising your awareness. For instance, digging a hole in the ground. You are digging a hole with a shovel, and isn't it amazing, as you slide the head of the shovel into the ground, how much dirt comes out with each scoop? The shovel only goes in the ground a short distance, and you come out with a full scoop of material every time. How do percentages work on your shoveling? How does gravity work? Does it matter whether the soil is dry or wet? How much rock and other debris are mixed in the soil? All these factors change how quickly you can dig the hole. Is it slow going in? Is it fast? Is it light? Is it heavy? Now how many different things are going on while you are just digging a hole? Where does your mind go as you are digging the hole? You can take your mind anywhere! Can you see how easy it works? It is a simple practice of grasping something out of everything you do no matter what it is! Can you imagine if someone asked you what you did today, and you told him or her, *"I DUG A HOLE!"* I experienced the coexistence of gravity within the depth of a distance I was digging, and this was going on, and that was going on, and it got heavier and lighter as I dug. I got to experience dense matter, and I got to experience light matter today. I got to experience the way it made my body feel as I dug. Don't you think they would believe you were crazy? All they saw was you digging a hole!

What is your level of consciousness? That is why certain people never find certain activities mundane! How many times can you clean a floor with a toothbrush and still feel the need to go back and do it some more? They are constantly getting something conscious out of everything they are doing!

Practice, practice, practice! Start practicing the art of getting something out of every moment or adding your consciousness to the experience of every moment. Your soul is absorbing everything that is going on. Your subconscious mind is absorbing more than your conscious mind is, and your conscious mind is the least active in all the activity! That's why we say raise your consciousness! Just raise your percentage a little bit. The percentage of your conscious mind is lower than your subconscious or your superconscious mind. Raise your percentage of consciousness. Realize you have more control of what is going on around you instead of choosing to misfire all over the place.

Theoretically speaking, you already know everything! You just can't remember because you are connected to all sentient beings, all beings that exist, and all beings that exist through the energy fracturing from SOURCE! Technically speaking, you know everything that SOURCE knows! At the same time, you are SOURCE experiencing everything SOURCE is experiencing about itself. There are just certain aspects of sleeping that is going on, so you can be in the action of experience. Or you can be in the action of experiencing yourself.

If you know all things, what is the best way for you to know or acknowledge the fact that you know all things? Do you temporarily forget some things? And as you remember them, will you have an appreciation that, at some point, you knew all things? That is what SOURCE is doing! You know all things in the ultimate reality level of speaking, since you are connected to all things, and you are SOURCE. You know all things in the ultimate reality and superconscious level. But by descending to a level like this worldly realm, you live like you are sleeping. You have literally fragmented yourselves and screened yourselves away from ultimate truth so you can experience something. Or you seemingly experience new things. When someone else reminds you of those things, or a teacher teaches you something, all they are really doing is reminding you of something. Not everyone gets the teaching that is being taught. It might end up being a process for you! Did you understand calculus as a kindergartener? Isn't it better for you to say I just didn't understand that part of myself this time around? For some reason I must have set it up that way. It was to master a different skill. I'm not going to be distracted by being a brain surgeon this time around because I chose this time to be a mechanic, or a carpenter, or a life coach this time. What excites you in your life's existence?

Do you remember your life's existence? Do you remember what was going on a day ago? If you are like most, you can remember an event that happened, or how you felt about something, but you don't remember the whole day's experience. Why do humans discount the intelligence of another human being for what humans believe to be a lack of intelligence? Are they not as gifted as you are? Do they see things that you don't, or they don't understand at the same level as you do? We can guarantee that the being knows everything that you know; they just chose not to remember it this time around. There are things that you chose not to remember this time around. A brilliant brain surgeon does not know how to paint a beautiful landscape because he doesn't remember! This time around he chose for that talent to elude him or her. You choose it.

Human beings have chosen all they are experiencing in this moment. If you would grasp the connection factor, you would realize that you all are connected. The disconnection factor of this illusion is what causes all the problems. Could you imagine how the teaching profession would change just by getting that simple concept? There would be no passing or failing. What if they said, as you came into class, we are going to help you remember how to do this! I can guarantee that at one time you knew how to do all of this! So, let's help you remember! Where is the discouragement in that? Let's stimulate your memory! Let's help you remember you are connected to your conscious, higher self! Just maybe you remember more than we do, so let's see how much we can remember! Can you imagine how education would change? Not all are going to get it, but some will.

What did you not receive in your last experience, that this time you have set up the playing field, so to speak, to allow you to experience? What is it you are trying to experience? Do you think the simple-minded person who sits and smiles at everyone every day is not experiencing what they want to experience? Do they experience their experience to the fullest? Or is the genius who is miserable with their life experience more just because they are a genius? Who do you think is more distracted? That's a distinctive way of looking at different people - who is gaining more experience in your mind?

Truth and understanding brings acceptance and forgiveness. In some cases, humans have not set themselves up for expansion this time around for some reason.

Does anger and fear and resentment run your life? Do you allow others to experience what they are trying to experience? Have you ever thought of it that way? A lot of people can't wrap their minds around expansive topics. They are so stuck in the illusion that binds them. They don't believe in anything that goes beyond this life. They are paranoid, they are angry, and they are fearful that some agenda has been set up for them. So that experience will grant that agenda, or it wouldn't happen. It takes place because some agenda has been set up, even if it is sometimes by example. What better way to encourage someone to expand their life's existence than by being an ignorant, angry person on this planet. You say you do not want to be that way. That is remembering by default. Sometimes that was the agreement.

Does someone bother you now who didn't in the past? Were you just like them and you didn't recognize that behavior? Now you have changed your life, and they bother you to no end. You can't stand to be around them. What a better way for you to see how it works. The more you expand, that person is just reminding you of how expansive your life has become. Can you see that? It doesn't mean you should take it; it just reminds you of your experiences. You are not going to take it this time around.

If that is difficult, it is because truth and understanding brings along with it expansion and acceptance. In most cases humans have not set themselves up for expansion this time around. Perhaps you wonder, now why would anybody not try to expand? Expand beyond the fear and anxiety that is holding them back? Do they think that way about everything? If they aren't thinking a certain way in the first place, do you think they think any way at all? What way are they thinking? Most can't even wrap their minds around any of the expansive topics. They are so stuck in the illusion that binds them. They don't believe in anything past this life's experience. Some agenda has been set up for that experience to grant that agenda. And that is hard to grasp. Most people's minds will never go towards that way of thinking. Most human's thoughts will never go to the expansive topics. They are so stuck in the illusion that binds them. They will never believe in anything past this life, even if it is by example. What a better way to encourage someone to expand than by being the most ignorant, angry person on the planet, even if someone else says I do not want to be that way! That is the agreement by default, and sometimes that was the agreement.

I surely can demonstrate to you how expansive you have become if I am the ignorant person that is always popping up in your life. You catch a glimpse of them here and there, and you think to yourself, *gosh darn, I can't handle being around them more than 15 minutes!* They are a wonderful reminder to you that you are expanding because they could be around all the time. At some point there was no problem with them being there all the time, and it was perfectly normal for you. Maybe you were ignorant that way, so that person didn't bother you that much. The more you expand, the more that person is just reminding you how expansive your life has become! That might be part of the agenda!

It is the same thing that is going on with SOURCE. SOURCE is learning and expanding by example, by contrast, and by experience. How do you know you are the light without the darkness? It all comes into play.

The role you are playing now, and the role others are playing now, are for all to expand. Are you playing your role perfectly? Are they playing their roles perfectly? Does recognizing something in someone else give you pause in your life to think differently? Does your being recognize that? There is always an agenda going on. Can you step yourself away from falling victim to another's perspective or agenda, so you can influence your experience by altering your viewpoint in every moment? In other words, are you staying centered amidst all the distraction? Not just the environmental distractions, but also the people who are around you?

Are you calm through the whole process even when a person literally strips you naked in front of everybody by yelling and screaming at you? Do you realize you are SOURCE, and you are all things? Do you send the harasser calm, peace and understanding to use in their life because they are lacking it? Do you choose to create your own experience of now? Are you gaining experience out of every moment of now?

How about the person who is so happy in their life, that they are always positive about everything? They are bubbly, and it always makes you feel good to be around them. Don't you just want to join them? That's all right because that happens too. Haven't you ever been influenced by the enthusiasm of a child that has just walked into a room? You are sitting at a table, and the spoon is the coolest thing they have ever seen! It's a spoon! It's round up here; it's straight down here. I can use it to pick up food, I can stick it on my nose, I can put my tongue on it, and it is cold. Just give a child a spoon and watch! All that just out of a spoon! Have you ever looked at it that way? By joining in the enthusiasm of the child, you change your perspective of the moment.

Do you think the child is getting the same experience you are? You are both sitting at the table. How about when the child decides to stick their hands in the potatoes? It looks just like clay. Man, can I have fun with this! Meanwhile, you are screaming don't touch it! Don't touch it! Why don't you stick your fingers in the mashed potatoes? It really feels kind of good. How much perspective are you getting out of every moment? There is nothing more fun to touch than Jell-O! I mean come on! What is Jell-O? It jiggles, it's sticky, it tastes good, and there is no child on the planet that is going to just stick a spoon into it! They are putting it on their face and everywhere else. Steak is fairly boring, but with mashed potatoes and Jell-O a child is in heaven! The spoon is so cool! How many people sitting at the table are missing that? Or are you one of those that are concerned about the mess that is going to be made? What is your perspective of the moment? Do you see the moment? You can choose to start seeing moments in your life, and when you see them, start adding one more experience to them. That is a step towards enlightenment.

Any time you can add an experience to anything in your life it is a step toward enlightenment. That is what you are doing!

You are here on the task of enlightenment! You are being a teacher and a seeker of more knowledge and enlightenment. Most of the questions that you ask yourself concerning this are just another rung on the ladder. You are on your way. Are you asking the right questions? Do you use all that the universe has to offer you? Do you realize that all things around you work in agreement and process? Are you tuning yourself into them?

Modern science has changed the use of the elements in our lives. We no longer line up our houses to catch the sun's rays. We no longer use the elements for our benefit. We wonder why we can't heat our homes efficiently. Why did the early civilizations flourish? They didn't have the technology we have today! What is it that we are missing? Are we at a disadvantage because of the knowledge that we have?

Does the influence of the illusion completely cover the reality? Why is it that we fight over whose opinion is right? What are we doing as humans? Do you recognize that? Take a moment out of your day and add one more moment to your experience. Soon you will be on your way to complete enlightenment. Enlightenment of your being.

Brad & Kasey Wallis | *Who You Are Being*

Twenty-Three ~ Circumstantial Beings and Dimensions

Since we have given you ideas to think about, let's share another concept: circumstantial beings and the dimensions they reside in.

This may seem confusing at first, however if you seriously consider it, there are beings that sit in what are called circumstantial dimensions, and those beings are what bring you and afford you the opportunity to experience the circumstances in your life.

For instance, you park your car in your driveway one evening, and in the morning when you get up your car is dead. There is no juice in the battery. You wonder to yourself how could that be? You haven't had a problem with that battery, and there were no signs that it was going to go out. Yet, because of the circumstances around the fact that the battery was dead, you had to change your plans for the day. By changing those plans, it afforded you the opportunity to experience something that you would have missed had you gotten up in the morning, gone to your car, and driven away. Circumstantial beings brought to you the circumstances that you were afforded to experience that day in your life.

How many times does something like that happen, and we get upset? We tend to think it is just coincidence, but most of the time we don't give it any thought at all. This conversation is about the circumstantial beings that sit within the circumstantial dimensions.

Sometimes in our daily lives things seem to be strange or completely out of sorts, but we have no explanation for them. Could it possibly be that your circumstantial beings are affecting something in your life? Are your circumstantial beings trying to show you something? Circumstantial beings can manipulate and play with colors and shapes. Of course, your colors, your shapes and your circumstances differ according to who you are since each human's circumstances are different.

The fact is there are beings in this universe that dwell within the dimensions that deal with the circumstances that each of us get ourselves into in each moment of each day of our life.

There is a dimension of beings that work very specifically in trying to set up the circumstances for human's requests that we send out into the universe. In other words, it's like this little dimension of workers that the universe says, *"Okay boys! This request has come in. You guys go out and set up circumstances for it."* That is all they do. They line up circumstances for people. You have your own group of workers that work on your circumstances just for you and they are doing this all the time. From the moment you get up in the mornings and start your day, the newspaper was there to meet you at the door because they had worked to make sure that the newspaper was there to greet you in the morning. They line up the circumstances to get you to work, whether or not your day goes smoothly or somewhat disjointed, and they help put into place what we would consider to be strange or coincidental. They really aren't strange or coincidental; it is just part of the alignment for the requests that we have put out to the universe. Do you remember the requests you send out every day to the universe? What is amazing is that there is beginning to be more and more people on this earthly plane that are starting to recognize these circumstances.

Human beings, as they work on expanding their knowledge and their understanding, begin to see these beings as they go throughout their day. At first it can be a little startling, but once you calm yourself down and realize that it is not going to cause you any harm, it is actually very peaceful and comforting. One should release the fear of it. It is always there; it is supposed to be there. This is just another being that is in one of those dimensions that we, as humans, are either not aware of or seemingly take for granted.

Circumstantial beings will not communicate with you verbally; all they do is set up circumstances for you in your life. That is how they communicate. That is what they do. So, you have to look for them and piece together the circumstances. That is their form of communication. In other words, they might be communicating to you through music, or they might be communicating to you through art. If you look at a piece of artwork, does it speak to you? Does it make a statement to you? Are you drawn to one thing or another through this artwork? Those circumstances were set up for you to receive that through this situation. That is how the communication works.

Do you hear a song during the day that, for some reason, just seems to tear at your heartstrings, or makes you feel a certain way? What do you think it was, or who do you think it was that made you feel that way? Once again, it is the circumstantial beings that have set this up, so you can recognize that. What is it then that it made you recognize? There are so many things in our lives that we take for granted, or things that happen in our lives, and we don't have an answer for them. These are the circumstantial beings that are afforded to each of us as human beings.

Circumstantial beings communicate to you through sound, color, and movement, and whatever they do will stir an emotion within you. That is their communication process with you. It helps you to become more aware of your emotions in your heightened state of awareness.

Dimensional beings in other areas of the universe do not communicate verbally either. There is no language where they are. There is language on this earthly realm, but there is no language where they are, so how else do you communicate with them? Dimensional beings have been hidden throughout your existence for a long time, and once you become aware of who they are, what they are, what they do, and the tasks that they perform, then your awareness will become heightened.

Human beings, at points in their life, lacked the capacity to match the frequency that these beings live in and exist, and we have a hard time acknowledging them. But for highly in-tuned individuals, you can start to sense that they are actually there. Once you start recognizing them, it will become more of the norm in your life. Pay attention to strange circumstances in your life. Those circumstances will offer you the opportunity to see and to experience a marvelous opening in your life. You will begin to recognize, and you will begin to see the circumstances that go on in your life that you are completely unaware of.

This is one of those awakening processes that an enlightened being goes through in their life. How aware do you become of the circumstances that go on in your life? How aware of the circumstantial beings are you that influence your life? Once you recognize them, and once they have become generous enough to show themselves to you, you need to acknowledge them and thank them for coming. Thank them for being there. Thank them for exposing themselves to you and ask them to keep showing up and controlling the circumstances in your life. These beings are anxious to communicate with you, and they can't do it without your permission.

Too many human beings are under the impression that a spiritual being is going to come and talk to them, but that is only one type of being. They do come and talk to you, but this is another type of being that we are in this conversation, bringing your attention to.

There are many other dimensional beings that are out there that don't speak. They use other ways to communicate with us, and because human beings are speaking beings, we miss that.

Human beings keep waiting for something to manifest itself to them in the room, and humans miss all the other messages that are out there. We have five other senses in the human body that we very seldom are even aware of, and those are the way they are going to communicate with us. This is actually a better way of communication because it triggers emotion, and that is the best way to get a message across.

Use the prospect of recognizing and seeing these beings and what they can do for you in your daily life's existence. We can assure you that once you see them and recognize what it is they do for you in your life, you will be amazed you were not aware of them before. Circumstantial beings. Yes, they are out there.

Twenty-Four ~
How Do You Master Your Teachings?

As you go through your life, and you begin to grasp your mastery, and you begin to want to be the teacher, and you desire to learn how to pass on the truths to others, or choose to help another human being remember the universal truths that are out there, you also begin to learn that there is only so much that you can do, especially for those that don't do in their life.

You certainly can do by demonstration, and you can talk about connection and disconnection, positive and negative, and doing and not doing. Others will always do, and others will always don't, and you must respect the choices of others. That is their experience this time around. One can remember that they are experiencing a single aspect of themselves. There will be those who will experience something, and there will be those who will experience nothing. You can realize that they will be having a totally different experience in their life the next time around.

You are educated through different contrasts of your life that you experience. It is only through the contrasts that you experience. Otherwise your life would always be the same. What do you experience through that?

Sometimes in families, for instance, you will find that there are siblings that are both extremely talented and gifted. For some reason, one of the siblings decides not to use his or her gifts to their fullest potential. Others who look at that experience are constantly asking the question as to why? We would say that the individual is experiencing exactly what it is they are going to experience this time around. There is a difference in the souls that are there. Each will experience what it is they plan to experience. Just like you in your life and your experience process. You are going to experience what it is you are going to experience.

Ask yourself a simple question: what do you see yourself as? Usually this will resolve the question that is going on in your life. Then ask yourself if you want to change that, or do you choose to change that? Is there an understanding in seeing the difference between wanting and choosing? When you say that you want, you are then stuck in the state of wanting, and the universe delivers that to you. So, you go through your life wanting until the day you decide to choose not to.

The only thing to fear is fear itself. How many times have you heard that comment in your lifetime? It is such a true statement! Those individuals who live in fear do not understand how it works.

People who are extremely positive in their lives, who are always looking for something else, or who are doers know that even if, by chance, they fail, they will do something else. Those people are always in the constant state of doing. By not accomplishing something, they've just realized that it wasn't going to work. So, they've decided to go and do something else, and they still try to accomplish what it is they're endeavoring to do. Too many times human beings will decide that if it doesn't work this time then they are finished, and they are done!

The speed at which your element moves, the temperature at which your element exists, and the frequency at which your element rises to, can change through your life. It can fluctuate. Some of the personality traits of your core existence can influence the manner at which you do things, or the speed at which you do things. As your element shifts in life, so do some of the aspects of some of the things that you do in your life. It gets back to that question: what are you going to do? I know that I am always doing! The speed of my element, and the temperature of my element, and the speed at which my element radiates effect the speed at which I'm doing. But those things should not take away the fact that you do things in life, especially when you attach your beingness to what it is that you do! Sometimes just doing that will give you the illusion that you're slowing your being down. You have spent so much time working on your being. You have spent a lot of your lifetime discovering who you are being this time around.

When human beings put themselves in the situation that they stop doing what they previously were doing in order to remember who they are being, it may be the only way that they could recognize who they are being. People are often so caught up in their doingness to even recognize that there was a level of beingness out there. You are too busy in your life being the cupcake, and you didn't take the time to realize that there was a tub of frosting sitting right next to your pan. So now, as a cupcake, you have saturated yourself in the frosting.

You are now realizing that you have spent so much energy and time in your life recognizing that you have been swimming in your being that you have realized that you want to get back to the doing. You now want to cover yourself in frosting. Covering yourself in frosting is a gentle process; you just can't slap frosting on the cupcake, or you would ruin the cupcake. You need to gently apply the frosting to the cupcake; you spread it absolutely flawlessly. The consistency of the frosting has to be correct, and the color of the frosting has to be correct. There is a marriage between the frosting and the cupcake. If you want the flavors to go together correctly, they have to be married together correctly. Just like the cupcake in the frosting, in your life you are trying to cover yourself with the experiences that will give you that sweet, savory feeling as you experience them.

When you undergo them, you want to teach others of the experience. Better not to get frustrated just because you're not an award-winning chef that has a network television series. This all takes practice. You are working on putting together an award-winning cake, and you are attempting to do it in one lifetime's experience. You are collecting all those things in your life in a single experience amidst all the other things that are going on.

If you are an individual who only wants to experience each experience individually, can you imagine how far you have to come? Where do you think the term icing on the cake came from? It is your beingness connected to your doing, and in the end, it tastes good!

There are a lot of things that are coming together. Once you acknowledge those things, you begin to work on those things, and it brings those things together. You become aware of the ingredients, and you become aware of how to mix them together. If it were to all happen instantly, what would be the joy in the process? If it happens instantly you don't appreciate it. You never do! SOURCE doesn't even appreciate it if it comes instantly; that's why SOURCE is doing what it's doing! It's the hard experiences that make it great! Human beings who have worked at their success through their lifetimes are the people that enjoy their life the most. The humans that have everything handed to them are bored with life, their lives are unfulfilled, and their lives are destructive.

Who are you being at this moment in your life? Are you headed toward never-ending expansion in receivership? Does your every moment in the eternal moment of now expand your being? Are you growing? Are you sharing? Are you growing as you share? Are you learning how to share? Are you learning to put the sprinkles on the frosting on the top of your cupcake? How about the whipped cream or the cherry? Those are the things that make you different than the others.

Do you always find what you're looking for? Do you always get what you are looking for? Whatever you think you are going to find is the perception that is going to take you to that experience no matter what you find!

If all you have coming out of an experience is great conversation, or you were enlightened, or you enlightened another, did you learn anything? Can you wait for the next time around? Did you learn to tweak what you were presenting to another, and did you learn from that? Do you go into your experiences, with them knowing of who you are?

Recognize the part of your being that is SOURCE with your open heart and soul. This time around you are going to add that onto what you are doing.

Are you walking in the light this time around? Are you spreading the light this time around? Is that what you do? Do others do it? Of course, they do, and good for them!

You are all on the same path of doing! As you wake up, and learn, and see, and grow, then teach! Teach others of the process! Teach others of the recognition! Teach others to be!

Twenty-five ~ Questions Humans Always Ask

Human beings always seem to ask the same questions. They ask questions that are tied into fortune, how they make money, how to make things work for them, and how to make relationships work for them. How do they become happy? How do they resolve problems with their children, their parents, a loved one, or their spouse? Humans continuously ask a lot of those same questions that deal with empowerment issues, and the lack of understanding to the connection to SOURCE.

The first thing that is essential for humans to get in their heads and into their conscious awareness, is that they are not disconnected. Human beings are connected. Human beings have an endless lifeline connected to the creator of all things. Humans have forgotten they have a direct phone line, if you will, and they've gotten distracted with the static that is on the line.

Humans like to ask questions like how do I bring things to my life? How do I bring things that I want? That's where the trouble begins. Humans need to get out of the wanting. Humans need to get into the choosing factor. Humans don't realize that wanting is a state of being. You are in this state of wanting, so the minute that you want something, you have placed yourself in this state of wanting, or lack, and you will experience everything that you choose. Even though you unconsciously have chosen to be in the state of wanting—you choose that just by saying or feeling that you want something—it puts you into that state. Now so that we haven't lost you, let's say it again: just by claiming the statement or feeling the feeling of wanting something, you have just placed yourself into that state of being. You are being wanting! Do have fun with that experience for as long you choose it. When you say *I want this*, the universe says *okay have fun. Have fun with that state of being. Have fun with that constant state of wanting!*

Did you know that the dictionary describes the word 'want' as the following:
1. lack or be short of something desirable or essential.
2. *archaic:* a lack or deficiency of something.

Synonyms: lack, be without, have need of, be devoid of, be bereft of, be missing.

You are keeping yourself in a constant state of wanting in your life. I want love, I want money, I want a house, I want animals, I want what my neighbor has, I want what I see on the TV, I want, I want, I want, and you are getting exactly what you are declaring! You are the part of SOURCE that wants!

So many humans are in that state. So many of you have chosen that part of SOURCE. It's the wanting state. The wanting experience. You have declared it by stating to the universe I want! You have made the I am statement that you want! Can you see how powerful you are there? Humans miss that! Humans have completely missed that they have the power to make an I am statement in every moment in the eternal time of now!

You are making a statement and declaration to the universe and to everyone else about the state of beingness that you are in, in every moment! Whether it be conscious or unconscious, you are in a conscious state of declaration!

I am tired, I am happy, I am sad, I am

happiness, I am nourishment, I am content, I am resentful, or I am angry. Whatever it is that you are feeling you are being and experiencing, and you make a declaration of, becomes your beingness in that moment. That is an incredible truth to grasp. If you could grasp it, you would understand how powerful you are.

You get to be anything you choose in every moment of the eternal time of now. What do you choose? Have we just woken you up to that truth? You get to choose! If you say to yourself, *"I'm unhappy!"* We would say stop it! Stop! Choose differently! You might reply, *"Well, it can't be that simple!"* It sure is, because you have gotten yourself to this state now! Nobody else got you to this state! You chose it. Nobody else put you here. And if anyone else did put you here it is because you allowed their actions to influence who you are being. If you gave them that power, you gave them permission, and you still made the choice. You can stay there if you choose. Or you can leave or get out of it as soon as you choose that instead.

Your choosing must come from the core knowing and beingness of your soul. Realize that not only are you connected to SOURCE, but you are SOURCE! You are as much a part of SOURCE as your foot is part of you. That is how powerful you are. Despite all the illusion, you may have any experience that you choose.

Some people proclaim, *"Well I don't feel like I'm very wealthy because I don't live in a very big house, and I don't drive a very big and powerful car, and I don't have all the expensive clothes, or wear all the expensive jewelry."* You don't feel wealthy because you choose not to! The other stuff is all an illusion. You may experience anything that you choose in the eternal moment of now. What do you think it feels like to be wealthy? What does it feel like? I guarantee your soul is safe. Your soul is as safe as the wealthy person's is! Know it. Feel it. It is a continual state of being that you choose to be in, in the eternal moment of now. Everything else is an illusion.

You are confusing in your life what your state of beingness is with the doing that is going on around you. You are not a human being; you are a human doing! You've given into the doings and the goings on around you. You have lost your conscious state of beingness! That is a powerful message. Are you in a constant state of beingness?

What are you constantly experiencing? What part of SOURCE are you experiencing in this moment for yourself? How did you get to the state of your being that you are currently in? You approved it, or you wouldn't be in it! Have you fallen into the illusionary actions that are around you, and have those actions put you in your current state of beingness?

You can choose the same game if you believe it is going to lead you out of it! Have you forgotten? Have you figured out this is all just an illusion? All these terrible things that have happened to you here, they are just an illusion.

Does your collective experience of this time around alter your beingness? It is a very difficult truth for many to accept. Humans don't want that type of power in their life! Human beings do not want to be responsible for who they are! There is too much responsibility that goes along with being responsible! You can't blame anybody else but yourself. It hurts when you realize the reason that you are in the state that you are in. Of course, you wouldn't agree to be in the state that you are in, but you have, or you wouldn't be in it! You have agreed that that is your state of beingness! It's not good or bad, and it's not making a judgment call, it's just giving you the information about the fact that you choose to be in that state of being, or you wouldn't be in it! If you don't like your current experience, then choose to be in another state!

This is a very difficult decision and a very tough understanding for human beings. The beings that it is the most difficult for are the ones that are caught in the illusion. They are in the illusion of disconnection. For those that contain themselves in the illusion, that is their state of being, and they choose it, and there is nothing you can do about it. Only they can do something about it. Does your beingness hold you in a state of connection or disconnection? If you don't want to be disconnected anymore, great! Shift your beingness! Now choose states associated with being connected, or you may choose states of being, that associate with being disconnected. There are plenty of humans on this plane that are in the state of disconnection. They choose their state of beingness based upon the disconnection factor rather than the connection factor. That explains why humans are so dark sided. For some it's too difficult to grasp, and so they choose to experience what they choose to experience.

How do I make a change in my life? How do I handle it? The first thing to understand is what frequency level you are connected to. Are you finally at a new frequency level? Can you know and conclude, that likened frequency beings are on their way to help you? You will be okay. It's okay. You can move on.

Stay focused on your connection, stay focused on your state of being, stay focused on your energy frequency, request help from the universe, change your thought process, and the universe will deliver what it is you are requesting!

There are ways to improve areas in your life by staying connected. Connect to SOURCE and your state of being. Realize that you get to choose the state of being that you are experiencing at every given moment. Your state of being is your experience. You have the power to alter your experience or your perception. All answers come down to the same truths. Are you staying centered amidst all the distractions?

It's very hard for human beings to let go of something until they realize it isn't right. If the shoe still fits, you're still going to wear it until it doesn't fit any more or until it gets worn out. It is so hard to tell somebody to take off that shoe and toss it in the trash when it's brand new. Don't put it on again! Only the person who is the owner of the shoe gets to make that decision! That's why so many things that seemingly still fit, hold you in a certain state of being; there's nothing you can do about it unless you change.

You must have a reason to change. You must have a reason to throw out your wardrobe and get a new one. Too many things influence your state of being. Are you ready for a new wardrobe, or for a new pair of shoes? It's time to start letting go of some of those and start opening yourself up instead to the possibility of total expansion. Realize that you have no limitations, and there are no preset notions for you.

You may select a new state of being that you choose to experience, and it will open a whole new realm. When things just don't fit anymore, change them. There's no reason for you to be having a problematic experience extensively, when things no longer fit.

Many people, many human beings, would rather stay in the comfort of what feels easy because it's too hard to switch everything around. It's just too difficult to change your wardrobe; it's just too uncomfortable to change your shoes. I can assure you, your soul will be safe no matter what you choose.

Brad & Kasey Wallis | *Who You Are Being*

Why is it that human beings often believe that there's a race going on? There isn't a race; it's a process. As soon as people try something new and it feels good, they seem to think they then must jump in head first and go for broke to win the race.

Humans always want to have more than they can handle, but don't want to do anything about it.

Let me share some truth and I hope you will absorb it. You are GOD, you are the SOURCE of all things, and you are the omnipotent creator of all things possible that exist on every different plane and dimension that is possible. You are the never-ending expansion of everything there is! Are you ready for that?

Please go out and share that with others. When you teach other people that truth, then you teach yourself as well! It is necessary that humans appreciate the fact that they are connected to SOURCE!

The moment that you can recognize that SOURCE is the ultimate enthusiast, we can guarantee you that you will recognize your optimism through your enthusiasm. Enthusiasm should be a state of being! What a wonderful state of being to be in. Congratulations, you are a human being!

Learn to love yourself and all that you do. Discover giving to not only yourself, but to others as well. Take each day to understand that what you do affects the being that you are. Realize that you can think differently. Learn to create things in your life, and not react to them. You are a human being. You are a powerful being.

Recognize your doings and identify your being. Remember who you are, and the truth of how powerful you are.

Many blessings with your being.

Conclusion ~

By Julius

As you read, reflect, ponder, and contemplate all that is written in this book, you will find yourself going back time and again to re-read something that has you thinking, or you will finally understand what you were thinking about. The awakening process is different for everyone, just as it should be. The healing process is different also, because you are all different. This is most important to understand. Source does not need any two of you feeling, understanding, or experiencing the same thing in the same way.

As you awaken to the knowledge in this lifetime's existence, it is important to not just read this information and move on. Take time to absorb the information; to experience the information and be involved in a valuable part of the cycle. Spend time in the deepening of your absorption, reminding yourself of your own knowing. You are always so quick to move on. There is always the desire for more and more, without proper assimilation. This information will not serve you and turn into knowledge or wisdom if time is not spent in absorbing the contemplated thought of the reality that has been given to you by adding new emotion to it, and thereby creating a new process from there. Spend time thinking about the concepts and truths in this book. Take the time to contemplate and see how well you understand the principles that are being spoken of here. Share your ideas with others. That is all part of the healing that will go on inside you.

New information has been given to you, new in the sense that it is new to your thinking or understanding. And at the same time it isn't new because there aren't any new ideas or possibilities, it is just a remembering process. Hopefully, you have been stimulated into remembering. And by remembering, you are now able to implement the ideas in your life.

All being well, you can resonate with the knowing or acceptance that you are a light being. And that you are connected to everyone, which in turn means we are all connected to each other and all are Source. May you treat your fellow light beings with the same respect you have for yourself. That respect will eventually change things in this world. We are all One!

As you take steps in your life, please understand that every step is a movement forward. And that each step is a powerful one. There is no such thing in this life as a small step, any movement forward is huge. That is the journey. It is what you long to be doing. No one takes a larger step than anyone else. As long as you are moving forward, your steps are equal. Once again, it is the human mind that gets into the calculation of what is a big or a small step, into the judging that some advancements are more important than others. That is totally incorrect.

There will always be those who will comment that all you are taking is small steps, and that in itself is a derogatory comment! Why is a small step not the same as a huge step? Perhaps for the first time in your life, you didn't get angry while waiting in line at the supermarket when the checkout person was slow. The person in front of you had coupons, which they spent a lot of time redeeming, and you didn't lash out, you didn't get angry! That is huge! You actually figured out how to choose enough patience to not lash out at anybody in front of you!

So then what is a large step versus a

small step? What is the difference? What is the definition of a large step moving forward, versus the small step moving forward? You are still moving forward! Everything is in a momentum! Speed and ratio are illusions! You are the ones who feel the need to measure everything, yet none of it is measurable! For the person who is confined to their bedroom, their decision to move out of the bedroom into the living room is huge. They are not out of the house, but they have moved from where they were previously to a new location! That is momentous for them, from their perspective. They were in the bedroom just a moment ago and now they've moved beyond! Just because they can't get themselves up and out the front door does not mean that they are not making progress! The door is the next step on their journey! Applaud them for making it out of the bedroom! But most don't and won't - they say that's not progress. But they are making progress, do you see that? Who is to decide or measure whether they are making advancements or not?

Then there are people in this world who are counseling others, and they belittle any type of progression in their life. They are constantly telling the ones who are seeking their counsel, well, that's a small step, that's a little step, hopefully we will get you to take a bigger step in your life! The truth is, that step is no smaller than the step the counselor took that day. And this is just another way that human beings bury each another in the illusion process. They get more satisfaction out of burying one another! They get satisfaction out of the belief that they are less than, or they are not equal to. And, of course, there is the oft repeated lie underlying it all - there's no way you are capable of being Source!

These are continual little subliminal, subconscious statements and beliefs that you give to yourselves, but worse than that, you give them to others. You perpetrate the illusion of separation, instead of spreading the truth of the total greatness of everything.

You are Source, you are moving forward, everybody is moving forward, human beings are moving on to their next experience, or at least another level of their experience. Are you going to continue listening to those who will take you away from your empowerment or are you going to stride confidently into your next moment, knowing that in each moment who you are being is creating all that you wish to experience?

Once you understand that no one is better than anyone else, you will let go of the idea of judging your progress. If you have momentum forward, you are doing exactly what it is you are supposed to be doing in this life's existence.

Learn, grow, develop, understand, become blissful in all you do. No matter what you do, you expand Source. So go out and expand yourself. Go out and experience all that you want to experience in this life. Keep moving, shifting, changing, growing and you will find every moment a moment of bliss!

How aware are you of your emotions? Are you aware of the steps that you are taking in your life? Are you aware that you are healing yourself, and that you are awakening that knowledge inside of you?

Self-awareness is the basis for all understandings. You will never know Source until you know yourself. Source lives inside of you and all around you, but if you do not go within to define the Source that is you, you will never be able to reach out to the Source that also lives outside of you. For having once gained recognition of the power of self, you then have a whole new perspective of the total beauty of all that has been created. To know oneself is to know Source, to be it in the moment of Now, according to your knowing! That is all you need to be doing. Then with each new experience you get a broader perspective. That expands Source. What a beautiful cycle to be in, what a beautiful ongoingness to be on. For at the beginning of all, there was Source looking onto itself, onto the knowing of the Source it was and is and looking to all the possibility of eternity and now. And you are the ones bringing those possibilities into experience!

Learn to love yourself and all that you do. Learn to be giving to not only yourself but to others as well. Learn to think differently. You are a powerful being. Learn to create things in your life, not react to them. Recognize your doings and recognize your being. Go through life seeing things differently. Don't ever forget who you are and just how powerful you are.

Take each day and see that what you do affects the being you are. Good luck with your being!

We wish to leave you with the expanded mind, with the desire to remember more, to challenge yourself to reach beyond your limitations to no limitations, and to accept all possibility. But most of all, allow others the same gift. There is no end to you, there is no end to the moment of Now, and because of that aspect you will be more. You will be part of what you thought of a moment ago. And so on... Be well, you most beautiful light beings. Be well in the knowing that we will continue, and you will continue. Find bliss in all you contemplate and that which others contemplate. We look forward to your very next thought, for that expands us.

Let that bliss carry you back to Source and the knowing and remembering of the

All.
    As it will be!

Julius

Made in the USA
San Bernardino, CA
21 December 2019